# ZARATHA'S EPISTOLARY

# ZARATHA'S EPISTOLARY

LUAN RAMA

ARCADIA

Translated by Miranda Xhilaga

Edited by Elizabeth Wade, Diane Carlyle

First published 2019 by Arcadia
*the general books imprint of*
Australian Scholarly Publishing Ltd
7 Lt Lothian St Nth, North Melbourne, Vic 3051
Tel: 03 9329 6963 / Fax: 03 9329 5452
enquiry@scholarly.info / www.scholarly.info

ISBN 978-1-925801-74-3 HB

ISBN 978-1-925801-75-0 PB



*Cover design:* Wayne Saunders

# LUAN RAMA

Luan Rama, born in Tirana, Albania, in 1952, is a scholar, filmmaker, editor and writer. He graduated in journalism from the Faculty of Political and Juridical Sciences, University of Tirana, and subsequently specialised in filmmaking and communication in France, at Paris VII Denis Diderot University.

His career spans more than fourteen years as a screenwriter of award-winning feature films, documentaries and cartoons for Albanian cinema studios.

From 1996 to 1997, he was editor of the French-language newspaper *Le Courrier International* (Paris) and he continues to contribute articles to both daily newspapers and Albanian revues.

He has also been a distinguished diplomat, who served as an ambassador of Albania (1992–2005) in Paris, Lisbon and Monaco. He further served as an Albanian cultural representative in Paris (1997–2003) at both UNESCO and the international French language organisation, OIF (La Francophonie).

Luan Rama has written thirty-eight books, including novels, short stories, poetry, correspondence, essays and historical works. Many of these explore linkages – historical, cultural and personal – between Albania and Europe, especially France. Among them are politico-historical works on General de Gaulle, and on former French President François Mitterand; studies on Greco-Albanian poet Jean Moréas, a founder of French Symbolism, and on Omer Kaleshi, a modern Albanian painter; essays on poets Jean Cocteau and on Arthur Rimbaud; and a novel on dancer Isadora Duncan's 1913 sojourn at the Albanian resort town of Saranda.

A number of his literary works have been published in France, including two volumes of poetry, *Territoires de l'âme* (Territories of the Soul) and *Couvrez-moi avec un morceau de ciel* (Cover Me with a Piece of Sky); the essays *Le long chemin sous le tunnel de Platon* (on the fate of the artist during the totalitarian era in Albania) and *Pont entre deux rives* (on Franco-Albanian linkages); and studies on Kosovo-Albanian painter Valdet Hamidi, and on French archaeologist Léon Rey and his pioneering work at the ancient Greek site of Apollonia, in Albania.

Luan Rama has been awarded many honours, for distinguished service to his country as well as for excellence in writing. These honours include: the Naim Frashëri Medal (Albanian civil award) in 1986; the European Award of ADELF (the French Language Writers' Association), for *Le long chemin*, in 2000; the Grand Officier de l'Ordre National du Mérite (French civil award, presented by then President Jacques Chirac) in 2002; and the Personality of 2014 of La Francophonie (presented by the Albanian Ministry of Foreign Affairs).

He lives in Paris, where he currently lectures on the history of literature and geopolitics at the Institute of Oriental Languages and Civilisation (Inalco).

Thus he set forth, and thus he had me enter the first of circles girding the abyss. Therein, as far as one could judge by list'ning, there was no lamentation, saving sighs which caused a trembling in the eternal air; and this came from the grief devoid of torture felt by the throngs, which many were and great, of infants and of women and of men.

(Dante, *Inferno* IV)*

---

* All Dante quotes are taken from *The Divine Comedy*, translated by Courtney Langdon, Cambridge: Harvard University Press.

# INTRODUCTION

Zaratha is a small island on the shores of southern Albania, situated in a shallow lagoon, covered with greenery – bushes, cypress trees and the tallest pines – so beautiful, as if it were a piece of paradise. Behind a narrow strip of land stretches the sea; on the other side, just beyond the shore, stands a watch tower for the prison officers and, a couple of hundred metres away, as if separated by a little drawbridge, is a village with a church and a bell tower that can be heard during the Sunday Mass. A bell that made a deafening noise. Some say that it was hit by a bomber plane belonging to the British Allies. Others say that God became angry with that church, and the sound of the bells has never been the same since.

A group of prisoners has just settled in the old, medieval monastery with a large courtyard and interior walls decorated with zoomorphic and geometric Byzantine figures dating back to the twelfth and thirteenth centuries. The church, with a dome, shaped as a crucifix, is complete with a narthex, a portico and a bell and it harbours a large tile slab written upon in Byzantine letters, which has served as a protective cover for a sarcophagus. It is thought that it is the tomb of Duke Argiro Karadza, sent here at the time by the Byzantine Emperor. The church has many beautiful frescos and a large iconostasis. The last monk died a year ago, but after his death the priest was dismissed on the pretext that the island was now considered a military zone by authorities always on the lookout for a possible enemy attack. After the last Mass, the priest, along with the villagers who came by boat, were forced to close the church's heavy door behind them and leave. However, the priest had vowed to return as 'no one could oppose God's will'.

Located just 300 metres from the shore, the island is filled with wild rabbits that swarm everywhere. Near the monastery, where the political prisoners sleep, on the other side, there is a lieutenant's cabin where you will always find three soldiers as well, all holding loaded guns. Only the bats can break the silence of the night, flying in and out. At times, bats would crash against the monastery windows and, one night, one of them broke one. Winter was approaching, so the prisoners were forced to replace the broken glass with some cardboard. Apart from the weak bulb at the top of the officer's cabin, the flickering of a candle that died late at night was the only sign of people living there, convicted men, most of whom were in agony.

Not far from the monastery is a cemetery with scattered tombs. The biggest and tallest of them all is that of a nobleman by the name of Karadza, known for his remarkable role in the wars against the Ottomans in the early nineteenth century. Further down is the tomb of Marigo Posio, the woman who is said to have embroidered the flag that Ismail Qemal Beu raised in Vlora on what is known as Independence Day, on 28 November 1912. A little further down is the beautiful grave of a young woman from a well-known family of the region and, because the girl visited the island often with her father and loved the place, when she died, her father brought and buried her here. It is surrounded by iron bars and its headstone reads:

> O passer-by, do not be surprised. Where you have been, I have been and where I am, you will be!

# THE FIRST LETTER

A heavy thunder-clap broke the deep sleep within my head, so that I roused myself, as would a person who is waked by force; and standing up erect, my rested eyes I moved around, and with a steady gaze I looked about to know where I might be. Truth is I found myself upon the verge of pain's abysmal valley, which collects the thunder-roll of everlasting woes.

(Dante, *Inferno* IV)

29 May 1957

Dear Bruna! It has been two months since they brought me here. I feel well and it is certainly the fresh air and good climate that have made the difference. The sun and the sea breeze have given me strength and I do not feel any chest pain as I used to before. Had it not been for Beso, my high school student, I would still be languishing in the dark and damp cells of Burrel.

You don't know him. He was one of my best senior students while in Shkodra; I was very fond of him. He lived not far from our house, before moving to Parruca. Fate would have it that after the war, he came to live in Tirana and hold the position he was in that would enable him to let me endure the rest of my punishment here. I saw him in the courtroom the morning of my sentencing. He stood behind others and silently stared at me with a sorrowful look in his eyes. However sad, he could not go against 'the Almighty'.* And yet, he found a way to help me.

* Coded word referring to the dictator of Albania.

On the island of Zaratha, for the time being, there are only ten convicts, but rumour has it that they will bring others. Everyone here is sick, most suffering from tuberculosis or other serious illnesses, and they feel absolutely hopeless. In fact, Petro, one poor old man, prays to God day and night to take him as soon as possible, because he can no longer endure the aches and pains of his heart and body. He is one of those who fought in World War I, among French troops and battalions across Shkumbini and The Stone of Kamja; he is one of those who fought against the White Russians who brought the King from Belgrade to fight Fan Noli. And after that, he fought in World War II. It was then his Calvary began, as nobody was interested in those who had served the country.

To stand against the Almighty, to speak against him, one would have to pay a grievous price. But Petro does not lose hope. 'A new day will come', he says. 'I won't be here, but you all will.' All political prisoners … Sazan is an architect and has studied in Paris, but since joining the group of independent MPs demanding a democratic Western system, as we have seen happen across Europe, he was captured and convicted.

Not far from my pallet is Vangjeli's. He is a hard-core nationalist who participated in the Mukja Conference.* He also fought for freedom, but after the war, everything went downhill for him. When the Germans arrived, the Albanian Government appointed him as a senior official at the Ministry of Finance. When the German Army fled, he did not leave as many others did but held the fort. And yet, he was imprisoned on charges of collaboration. But he suffers from a liver disease that has progressed here, as it seems he now has cirrhosis. Doctors are of the opinion that he will not be around for long so they have brought him here to die.

Sefer, a bed further down, was the commander of a partisan squad and fought hard for the cause but, because he did not kill certain nationalists as per the orders from above, he was considered one of their collaborators.

---

* An infamous national forum aimed at uniting Albanian political forces against German occupation, held in August 1943. Decisions and a committee formed at this conference were not recognized by the Albanian Communist Party and the allies of Enver Hoxha, the Yugoslav delegation, dividing the country at a time of great need for unity.

He almost never speaks and is rather sad because he has left behind his wife and toddler as well as his old mother. He walks up and down like a monk all day and I feel sorry for him, as he is a good and just man. At times, he sings a sweet, sad song, a living nightmare of a song, the typical sad stories told where he comes from, the Kurvelesh Mountains …

Xhevo is the youngest of us, a charming, tall boy. A few days ago, he was told that his mother had died, and he wanted to go to her funeral. He asked for permission and then wrote a letter to the prison command in Tirana, but never got a reply. He weeps in silence. It has been days since he last said anything or ate. He blames himself for her death. There is a large gash on the side of his forehead and the wound is closed, but it seems to have left a life-long mark. One day I asked him who had done this to him – the interrogator? But he replied, 'I don't know!' – and ran his hand over the wound as if perceiving it for the first time. He is lost, poor soul …

Xhako has pretty bad health but strong views; he has just come out of a two-year period in solitary confinement. They caught him trying to escape Albania via Pogradec. They tortured him fruitlessly; they got nothing out of him.

Stavri, a man in his forties, is the most charming, because he has a jolly nature and with his jokes he tries to take away the sadness that has fallen on us all. He fought as a partisan but was from a well-to-do-family. 'We will all die one day, we and they – all!' – he often says … A bullet, courtesy of the last war, still resides in his body, between his heart and his shoulder. Another has left an big open hole in his thigh. The wound in his shoulder had been closed for a long time, but somehow, it got infected in the cell and now has become an urgent issue …

Petro is here too, a former Noli supporter, as well as Kamberi, 'the Poet', as we call him. Sometimes he is happy, but more often he behaves like a monk. He locks himself up for days in his cell and does not speak to anyone. Poor Kamberi suffers a lot, but he is also crazy. He was brought here because he sent a letter to the Almighty accusing him of acting as an absolutist king, like Louis XIV of France, and saying that Albanian literature could not be dominated by Stalinist dogma. They say that the

Big Man was so upset by the letter that he ordered Kamberi's eyes to be wrenched from their sockets!

Up until now, we haven't seen a single wave on the sea. The oarsman, Rrapush, a seventy-year-old who lives up in the village, comes every day to bring us bread for the day, a single little piece each, and some kind of soup that tastes of nothing, and a few olives. When I see him from afar, I follow him with my eyes all the way – he reminds me of the ancient Charon and the river Acheron that flowed towards the Kingdom of the Dead. Life here is strange: instead of thinking of my future, I think of old Greek and Roman myths and it feels as if we were living some of the famous tragedies and dramas of classical times. It seems like nothing has changed! People wear the faces of Nero, Antigone, Cassandra, Circe, Oedipus, Heracles and Menelaus.

Remember that last afternoon, Bruna, when we were going to the movies? It was the last time. I was waiting right beneath the city clock tower. We were going to watch a French movie. You would be coming straight from home and I would be waiting for you. That morning you were wearing that violet summer dress you liked so much. There I was waiting, when suddenly, two officers, dressed as civilians, approached and asked me my name. They knew it alright. They told me to follow them. At first, I objected and said that I wanted to wait for you and at least tell you what was happening. But they were in a hurry and they forced me into a Jeep that was waiting with its engine running. At that very moment, I heard a voice calling me: 'Professor, Professor! What are they doing to you?' … it was one of my former students. Poor boy, he was looking at me with visible distress. 'Don't worry!', I said. 'It's nothing … it's a misunderstanding!' They pushed me into the car and at the last moment I saw him gazing at me terrified, worried for my life … At that moment the city clock struck and I knew that in just a bit you would arrive and wait for me. I looked back but you weren't yet there. You probably waited for me a long time. You must have searched for me everywhere. You must have cried a lot and you would not have been able to sleep. You, and my poor mother … On the other hand, I am glad that you did not see me being taken by force. That little scene would have upset you terribly …

Ah, Bruna, I remember so vividly the night they brought us here. We had no idea what was happening, where they were taking us. Perhaps to a dreadful unknown prison? They loaded us three by three into a boat and brought us here handcuffed, accompanied by armed soldiers. Rrapush had the boat. It was pitch black. Again, I thought of Charon rowing us down the Acheron River towards Hades and the Kingdom of the Dead. We could hear only the paddles slapping the water, the boat gliding through it and the sound of an owl.

And so, handcuffed, they pushed us out of the boat on to the land, towards a large stone building where we could hear our voices echoing. There was no one in sight. What was this? Was everyone asleep? Where were the inhabitants of this place? Where were the prisoners? Exhausted, we collapsed into sleep on a heap of straw. It was only the next day, when we woke up, that we realized that we had been thrown into an abandoned monastery, its walls covered in frescos depicting the faces of the saints and their acolytes. When we approached the gate and understood that we had been transported to an island, we began to breathe and forget the torture, the pain, the suffering, the ingrained anxieties of our near-death experience. We could not believe our eyes: before us was paradise itself – this island was an undiscovered gem of nature. Later we were told that it was the island of Zaratha …

It is interesting how cloudy it is here though. Perhaps it is the lagoon that gathers the clouds or maybe they come with the sea breeze. Occasionally, I lie down and watch the sky, the clouds. A miracle of nature, as they never stay the same. They come and go so fast, hang strangely, then disappear again … If I were an artist, I would paint them, but here I am a convict. One day I was lost in looking at this miracle of clouds when I felt a big boot kick my legs very hard. 'What are you looking at?', asked the guard, the gun slung over his shoulder. 'The clouds', I said. 'What's there to see?', he said sarcastically, and laughed like an idiot, walking away. Now, whenever he catches me looking at the sky, he says ironically: 'Hey, the clouds! Any news?'

Yet, as I lie here and gaze at the heavens, into that beautiful dance of clouds, I wonder to myself: If there were a God, surely he would not have allowed suffering here? I am not sure, I have started to doubt myself. Does God exist? Where is he? Oh, how I would like to believe! … I remember one day at the college when I was giving a lecture on Socrates' Apology, a student asked: 'Is it true that Socrates was condemned – and why?' 'Yes', I said, 'the great Socrates was condemned by the "nobles" of the city, the swindlers, the corrupt, and those who chased power to enrich themselves, because he always spoke the truth and was not afraid of truth. He always protected the humble and mistreated. He sacrificed himself so that his death would illuminate the truth …'

Last night, I dreamed of you, Bruna. It felt as if two hands lifted me from my bed and held me, lifting me towards the sky. And so, I was flying around, as if in a Carpathian drawing. Strangely, there were no stars even though I was aware of this phosphorescent light, perhaps from a moon hidden who knows where … and I went west. I felt as if I were riding on a cosmic cloud, heading towards some sort of brightness. It was the light of a star that became stronger, brighter, a beacon of fire, which drew me into another world. Was that you? … I was looking for you in that great radiance! … I would like to write much more to you, but in two hours Sotir's mother, who arrived suddenly, leaves for the city. I will have to be very discreet when handing this to her and hope that she will bring it to you as soon as possible.

I send you a big hug, my darling!

Fred, who lives every moment of his life with you in his heart; with you every moment

'*Dum spiro spero*' … 'As long as I breathe, I hope'

# THE SECOND LETTER

> We had set our steps within a wood, which was not marked by any path whatever. No green leaves there, but leaves of gloomy hue; no smooth and straight, but gnarled and twisted, twigs; nor was there any fruit, but poison-thorns ... Moans I heard uttered upon every side, but saw no person who might make them there; hence, utterly confused, I checked my steps. I think he thought I thought that all those voices were uttered from among those thorny trunks by people hiding there on our account.
>
> (Dante, *Inferno* XIII)

25 June

Dearest, your letter filled me with joy. I was particularly pleased to learn that my mother is still hanging in there. My poor mother! My incarceration has devastated her. I fear that her heart won't take it much longer; your love and care are my only consolation. Seeing Doctor Zia now and then, at the hospital, should do her good. You could even ask him to make a house call. He will be more than pleased to see her, as he is an old family friend. In September '44, during the curfew, we hid him in our house for five days. He is amazing and a well-respected man throughout the city of Shkodra.

Yesterday, the village priest arrived because it was Saint John's day, the name-day of the monastery. The boatman brought him early in the morning and it seemed as if he were in a hurry to finish the Mass as soon as possible.

What Mass?! There was no one there, no believers, no villagers, no one! The faithful, most of them elderly, were still waiting at the shore because one of the officers, himself a believer, had told them that they needed the permission of his commander to attend. 'But we want to honour our saint!', they protested. 'How can you cancel the Mass on the very special day of the saint?' But the soldiers allowed only the priest through and formed a barricade against the villagers.

Some of them would have walked through the water to get to the other side, if need be. Mind you, they would have just managed to keep their heads dry as the water is rather deep. But the soldiers did not care! However, the priest did conduct some sort of ceremony for the saint. As he was entering the beautiful little church embellished with its Byzantine frescos, his eye caught a little piece of paper pinned up by an old nail on the wall … a list of the prison rules, the nail piercing through a painted saint's outstretched hand. His eyes popped! He screamed so loud that one of the officers ran to find out what had happened. Had the priest gone mad? The priest pulled the nail out of the wall but didn't know what to do with it. He was indeed incensed but the officer, arrogant as he is, turned to him and ordered him to finish as soon as he could because no one had time for him and his silliness.

The priest hesitated, panting, but he was really scared of these men with automatic weapons ready to fire. Eventually, he made the sign of the cross in front of the frescos, the saints and Saint John, and read a psalm under the dome of the church. His voice pierced the very ceiling. The officer turned abruptly, because we had all gathered at the church's door, and screamed: 'Go! There is nothing for you in here! Get lost!' We stepped back … The priest continued to read: 'But whoever hates his brother is in the darkness and walks in the darkness, and does not know where he is going, because the darkness has blinded his eyes'. Then it all went quiet. He left, muttering to himself … 'Almighty God! Have mercy on them, for they know not what they do!'

And so, Bruna, he left as he came, with the waterman. We would have loved to accompany him as far as the water's edge, but the officer was still there making sure that no one made a step in his direction. We really couldn't do anything. We stood there in silence looking at the priest who was so enraged at the nail that had pierced the hand of the saint, recalling the crucifixion of Jesus … his hands and feet tied, nailed, fastened to that large wooden beam, left to hang there for several days. So insensitive, this nail on the wall, so hard to take for someone who has dedicated his life to Jesus.

He is surely aware of the times we live in, though. He knows all too well what happened to the Catholic Church hierarchy of the country, how priests and other servants of God were shot dead, how others simply disappeared and/or were imprisoned, and he probably prays that one day soon, the sky will fall on them …

When the priest was stepping into the little boat, I thought I saw Mother Mary. I thought of the day when we were listening on the radio I had brought from Turin, to that beautiful aria, Schubert's 'Ave Maria', sung so beautifully by our dear friend Giuseppina. Do you remember the concert that night at the theatre? What a marvellous night! I play that aria in my mind so that I can forget the world I live in now. I hear her voice, I see Mary and I imagine we are together, on this island, in the most beautiful cathedral in the world, where we search for each other's hands and, when we find them, we hold on to each other so tightly. Like in a heavenly song. Do you remember the Song of Shulamite, the Song of Songs, otherwise known as the Song of Solomon? The oldest love song and the most beautiful of them all? I sent you a few of its verses from Turin and you asked me to translate the whole thing …

> By night in my bed I sought the one / who my soul loves. / I sought that one, but I didn't find any trace. / I will get up now, and go about the city, / in the streets and in the squares / I will seek that one who my soul loves …

Yesterday, Sazan, the architect, was showing us his drawings of a bridge that could potentially link the island with the mainland. These are shallow waters because it is a lagoon, so one could easily build a low-cost bridge. He reckons that all you need to turn poor Albania into a tourist attraction is a bridge! He has drawn a bridge so beautiful, with gorgeous arches. In fact he went so far as to show it to one of the officers, who promised to help, but we haven't heard anything from above yet. They probably think that it is simply an escape plan! We will see whether someone from above might show a real interest … it would really mean something to the future of this place.

How much longer will I stay here, my sweet? Ten years, my entire sentence? Will they not show some mercy, to reduce my sentence and finally understand that I have never been a collaborator with the enemy and that the only thing I have ever done is to obey this system? Why do people in the West fight for democracy? Why is the freedom of the individual so dear, and life so good, why are science and technology so well developed, art and literature too? Everything is linked to the status quo.

But you know the answer all too well; I am not sure why I am telling you this. All I really ask is that one day, they show some mercy, some justice, because ten years is a hell of a long time! How can I live for ten years without you by my side, thrown upon this little island, away from the life we had started to build together? Ah, time … I long for a heavenly clock, the hands of which would move faster, which would make days and months go quickly, years too, and so the day of my return would swiftly come and I, like another Ulysses, of another time, after all this suffering, would walk the beautiful paved streets of my city to arrive on that doorstep … to push the door open and find you there, you and my poor mother! Ah my dear Bruna, this longing is killing me, it has me by the throat, it's suffocating me! Nevertheless, breathless as I feel, I envision you, because if I didn't – if I couldn't be with you in my dreams and my nightmares – life would truly be unbearable!

Now that I write, I have Dante's verses right before me and I am not sure why but I came to think of one of the greatest French artists of this century, Rodin. Perhaps because one of his greatest works, a rather curious sculptural fresco called *The Gates of Hell* was inspired by Dante's *Inferno*. I remember vividly the day when we visited this magnificent piece, with some students from class, on a three-day trip to Paris. It took Rodin thirty years of hard and persistent work to finish it. He passed away well before it was cast in bronze. I saw those gates and the work now re-emerges with all the magic and tragedy it carries. I stood speechless in front of it … Everything was there, even the entanglement of bodies as in Botticelli's paintings of Dante's *Inferno* that refused to take up colour … It seems that Botticelli had to go through the same creative path as Dante to give birth to *Inferno*. What a shocking image, especially when rain has fallen over the gates and when sun lights up all the touches of the master's hand, all the shadows of the characters, those convulsing bodies, as perceived by Dante who was himself a convicted man, forced to abandon his beloved home city of Florence, condemned to death. Portraits, arms, limbs, contortions of the human body, eyes that keep you imprisoned, the same desperate screaming mouths.

Yes, there was *The Gates of Hell*, Dante's shadow reflected in the sculptor's studio at Meudon, on the outskirts of Paris; many of the works he created there would later become well known, including *The Thinker* or *The Kiss*. And again they turn up on that great door, in that crowd of sinners who give expression to all the states of the human condition. A child alone in a corner, miserable and innocent, wondering naively why he is there at all, if his parents are there somewhere too. Further along, elongated heads that sometimes look like gargoyles. No, not imaginary faces but those of human beings, created by Rodin's own sculpting tools in the middle of feverish nights, sleepless nights, gripped and driven by the fever of Hell and the face of sin. Women who seem to be bare-arsed, erotic and tragic at the same time; people looking for their road to salvation in order to escape from punishment.

Rodin was also a sinner. And wasn't it another hell, the pain he went through for his girlfriend Camille Claudel, who went mad and was confined for many years in an asylum, forgotten by society but not by her body or her art? *Inferno*, in my view, is nothing but a meditation on the human condition in general. *The Gates of Hell* is much the same, as Rodin – like Dante – shows humankind the shocking condition of human society, which hasn't changed much over the years: fraud, theft, defamation, revenge, cynicism, thirst for power, money and glory, where the weakness of the human soul leads directly to crime. Rodin, just like Dante, tells much the same story, not through words but with his work tools – his sculptures representing entangled human bodies, like those featuring Ugolino, the tyrant of Pisa, and his killing of his innocent children, for which he stands eternally condemned in those gates.

Last night, I stepped out of the monastery and looked at the stars. There, Galileo appeared, old and wise, proclaiming the Earth's motion around the sun. I was imagining that singular scene, the man before the Court of Inquisition, the wretched Galileo, threatened with a burning at the stake, forced to deny his findings and beliefs. And as he was leaving, I could hear him whispering: 'And yet, it moves'. And I feel as if I constantly repeat these words because, my dear Bruna, things always do return to their ordained state …

After midnight, I lay again in my bed. It was full moon and the light that entered through the monastery's windows spilled over the apostles' and the angels' faces. It must have been soon after I fell asleep when I dreamed that one of the angels appeared before me, robed in purplish red, and asked me to follow him: 'Where are you taking me?', I asked. 'To the one you love', he said. And I followed him blindly. When I arrived, stunned, you asked: 'My love! Who brought you here?' 'Angels', I replied. I turned my head to show you my angel, John the Baptist, but he had already disappeared. I just wanted to lie down beside you, in your bed and take in, one more time, the aroma of your breasts. 'Come', you said, 'come my love, the love that burns inside my soul'. I curled into your belly, in a foetal position, as if I were a child, listening to your heartbeat.

'*L'amaro lagrimar* – the rain of bitter tears'

Finally, I want to write to you about Luigi, my high school friend, with whom I stayed for a month at the small citadel of Porto Palermo. Is he back? I would like to know what happened to him, as he was a wonderful friend. You did not get the chance to see the place where the political prisoners were kept, as they did not give the permission to come and visit. It is a fortress erected on a plot of rocky terrain, almost a small island connected to the mainland by a strip of land. Centuries ago, the Venetians built there a protective fortress for Ali Pasha of Tepelena – a place where he put a battalion of men observing movements in the Ionian and Adriatic coasts. I was always amazed at how two hundred people could be kept locked in the basement spaces of such a small fort; from the upper fortress, there were a few steep steps, the only side where the light of day and the sun could get through. Unfortunately, light failed to overcome the darkness in that place; we lived there in the half-dark the whole time, looking towards the steps' entrance, from where the sunlight might one day come. That's where I stayed with Luigi and talked about Rousseau and Diderot, Voltaire and Descartes, since Luigi had studied philosophy at the Sorbonne in Paris. We kept walking up and down the interior space, under vaults covered with inscriptions, with dates and names of people, seeing entire families, including children, pushed into a corner, living their miserable destiny. Yes, my love, there were children there too – incomprehensible though it is. What kind of wrong could they possibly have done against their country? It was really a scene from hell: in the middle there some kind of stone kitchen, and a place where women washed their clothes which would barely dry, because of the humidity and lack of air. People were like the inhabitants of another planet. Dante might have imagined such a place, but he would never have seen such a thing.

A month before my transfer, dysentery broke out and the guards were forced to let us outside. We were almost blinded by the sunlight. Luigi was quite ill, and I looked after him throughout the ordeal. I looked at his sunken eyes and pale skin and thought that I probably looked the same. It was the first time in months that I had seen the sea and the waves that hit the walls of the castle – a noise we could only hear from down there, without ever seeing the sea for a moment. It was unimaginably beautiful. Seeing birds again and hearing their cries was something utterly sublime. Ah Bruna, I do not know what happened to Luigi afterwards. Maybe he made it back to Shkodra? Let's hope so …

Fred, who misses you dearly

'*De nobis fabula narratur*' … 'This is our story'

* * *

A military aircraft flies low over the camp while another zooms rapidly over the island. Concerned, the convicts sitting outside look up, observing what seems intended as an intimidating show of strength. The rest of the convicts tumble out of the monastery to witness this strange and unexpected noise.

'What's going on?', one asks.

'Apparently it's finally erupted!'

'What?', asks Petro.

'The war!', murmurs Xhevo.

'What war?'

'The last of them all, the nuclear war … between the Soviet Union and America. The Third World War.'

'Why the last one?'

'Because afterwards the world will turn into a volcano crater … dust!', said Fred. 'Remember Hiroshima?'

His friend scratched his head but said nothing.

'Hiroshima! Hell on earth!'

'They say Russian ships are approaching Cuba from the Atlantic. Their ships carry nuclear missiles. Same with the Americans. They will be facing off against each other in no time!'

Petro seems to be deep in his thoughts about the war. The jets have now departed, and the island falls silent for a little.

'The world is sinking into the greatest tragedy of its history', says Fred sadly. 'Even Dante could not have imagined such an apocalypse.'

Meanwhile, from his lookout, the Bulldog turns towards the convicts, screaming: 'You human garbage, get in! What are you waiting for! …'

The prisoners stand for a moment, undecided.

An automatic rifle fires up, piercing the air.

The Bulldog laughs, howling: 'You stinkers … Cuba will win … Long live Castro! Long live Ho Chi Minh! Didn't you hear? … The cause you have all fought for is no more!'

And he fired his rifle again, aiming at the sky.

* * *

# THE THIRD LETTER

'Look where thou walkest! and see that with thy feet thou tramplest not the heads of us two wretched, weary brothers!'

(Dante, *Inferno* XXXII)

3 July

Bruna, my darling wife, tell me why I started translating Dante at *Paradise*? Why? Is it maybe because I dreamed of a better life, a happier life with you? I dared to dream a lovers' life, a life that would allow us to build our sacred family, with our children. I never told you that the translation of *Paradise* was brought up in court. The prosecutor was waving the manuscript in my face, shouting, 'What is this rubbish?' 'What is this good for, what kind of paradise are you talking about? What good does this do us? Don't you know that the real – the one and only – paradise is the one that this government is building for its people, the Proletariat's Dictature state? He spoke on and on, but finally I said to him: 'It is Dante's *Paradise* … it speaks to all humankind about the creation of a better and more humane society'. I had to protect my beloved Dante, Bruna. Dante would never have known that, someday, he would be put on trial in a small country on the other side of the Adriatic … Later, one of the members of the jury, who apparently had read Dante, signalled for an end to that conversation, because there would be university graduates present who had studied Dante in France and Italy, and it would be embarrassing for the court if it discussed the work like that

… However, keep my handwritten translation, darling, together with my other notes; we will need Dante later …

What do you think of the work I have done so far? Please show it to Lazer – he knows Dante really well and has read him in Latin, just like me. Ask him what he thinks about the last two sentences of the seventh song.

Oh, what am I saying really … better leave it. I no longer think of *Paradise*, the bit I have translated, I constantly think of *Inferno*. I have just started translating the first song. It is without a doubt one of the most beautiful things ever written by human hand. Give it, give it to Lazer, give him these few additional bits. *Inferno* is the strongest part of *The Divine Comedy* What a moment in history! How on earth was he able to fathom as he did the human world and what happens within one's soul, the hell within, men and their sins, their disgrace, a man's murderous instinct and his brutish feelings? And me? What kind of sin have I committed? Why am I here, and why are these other poor men, these friends who are such good fellows? Isn't my life here some type of hell, when you think of the months I spent under interrogation in that small, damp cell where it was so hard to breathe? Must we suffer? In the name of what, of whom? Oh Bruna, I want to live another life, the one we started together …

Do you remember that night I was telling you about Florence and the day I went to visit Dante's house, the place where the genius used to live? It was a large house made of stone, with small windows and a huge courtyard. It was my university friend from Florence, Antonio, who took me there. 'Come with me', he said, 'so I can show you where the creator of *The Divine Comedy* used to live, that stone house with the carriage entrance. Then he dragged me another eighty metres further and told me: 'Do you see this other house?' 'Yes', I nodded. 'This is where Beatrice used to live, Dante's girlfriend, the one he dedicated his work to!' … What a love story! They lived so close to each other, no farther than the distance from the start of the main street of Shkodra to the Big Café! I cannot possibly forget the verses he wrote for her. Yes, we know all about Dante's sonnets for Beatrice, but we know very little about his life and relationship with her. She was nine years old when they first met. His father sent him to his friend's house, a man called Folco Portinari, and there he saw Beatrice for the first time, as a ten-year-old. They became friends and then fell in love, a love that they got to experience for only a very short time. She died at the age of twenty-four; your age now. Her death devastated Dante. Later on, he became an important official of the 'White Guelph Party', as it was called at the time. But when the 'Black Guelph Party' came into power, Dante was forced to leave and so he began his exile, always moving from one city to another. But Beatrice remained his Morning Star. What a loss! For years to come, Dante would live with her image, would walk seeing with her eyes, would breathe for her, would revive her in his heart and he would make her whisper and tell him the world's love and pain. Did she possess some kind of divine power? Of course not! It was love that gave her grace and divinity. I often see you in such a light …

My dear Bruna! Yesterday, the guard saw me with my translated work and Latin vocabulary in hand. 'What's all this?', he shouted. 'Paper', I replied, 'a literary translation …' 'Of …?' 'Dante … *The Divine Comedy*!' 'And who exactly is this Danti who has come all the way to this little island of Zaratha? What "comedy"? You think this is funny business we do here?!' … He had never even heard of the genius's name! He called him 'Danti' but I corrected him … I then told him that they were love songs, that he had lived in the fourteenth century and that he sang them to Beatrice … that Dante was studied at all the colleges. In fact, that Jeronim De Rada was one who had translated a few of his songs. 'De Rada? – Albanian?' 'Yes, an Albanian of Arberia.' 'Aha, strange …', he murmured and left with a smirk on his face. The guard is not a bad person, he is simply an ignoramus, whereas the three other soldiers are savages. Between us, we have nicknamed one of them 'the Bulldog' because he looks like one with his big head; he kicks and screams at us all the time … But anyway, it was when I told him that Dante is studied in colleges around the country that he left me alone. And then I went for a little walk up to where the forest begins, because I am not allowed to go any further. The Bulldog would come after me screaming and shouting, and hitting me. I was sitting down thinking of you when I sensed a butterfly fluttering close and coming to rest on my shoulder. God knows why, but there were a good many of them there, enjoying the sunlight and the gentle sea breeze. Was it perhaps a gift from above sent to soothe my soul or a sign to remind me of your birthday, a day we always celebrated with our friends? It was a big-winged, yellow-spotted blue butterfly, very special. I stayed there for a while without moving, and when I simply turned my head to gaze upon her, I thought that perhaps you had sent her to me. I didn't want to scare her off; I wanted her to stay as long as possible. After a while, she spread her wings and took off to join her sisters, zig-zagging through the light wind. I would dream of this gleaming butterfly throughout the night and see her flitting around the angels' faces, then descending rapidly to swoop over our beds. As if concerned whether we were breathing or not. Then she came to sit on my pillow and rested with closed wings. Perhaps she wanted to sleep next to me – I was her chosen one … I chose to think she was you!

The day after, it rained. My friends stayed in but – who knows why – I wanted to be out there, looking at the heavy, dark sky. Soon enough I felt the rain on my face. For the first time I was feeling something different; it was quite lovely, as if a damp hand were caressing my forehead, my eyes, my lips and continuing down my cheeks and neck. I could feel the droplets penetrating my clothes on to my body, and it was so pleasurable. I am not sure why I was doing this. I just knew that it was you who occupied my thoughts.

Do you remember that day at Xhabiajt Road? It was sunny and all of a sudden, the summer sky opened and it started pouring down and we had to run for cover so fast! While we were running, the buckle of one of your sandals broke and you had no choice but to hold it in your hand and keep on running with one foot bare, laughing out loud, until we found cover. We were so happy! You were all wet and your dripping, long, curly hair wet my face. I gave you a quick kiss as someone else joined us under that roof. And then the sun came out and we left. Your hair looked so shiny and you kept on walking with one bare foot, holding the broken sandal. All the passers-by smiling … Ah, our Shkodra that I miss so much, just as Dante missed Florence up until the day he died. Florence, about which he wrote:

'We love Florence so much that we suffer just because of it!' ... '*Nos quia ... deleximus exilium patriamun iniste*'.

Before closing, I wanted to remind you of one of Dante's *Paradise* cantos where speaks to his Beatrice:

> 'O Lady, thou in whom my hope is strong, and who for my salvation didst endure to leave the traces of thy feet in Hell, I recognize the virtue and the grace of all the many things which I have seen, as coming from thy power and kindliness. From slavery to freedom thou hast drawn me in every way, and over every path, within thy power to achieve that end. Guard thou in me the fruitage of thy bounty, that thus my soul, restored to health by thee, may, when it leaves my body, please thee still!'

My dear, in Dante's book *A New Life*, a kind of autobiography about his spiritual renewal, he recounts how his youth was filled with joy. He writes about how this love was born and how it eventually became so exhilarating and sovereign to his soul. I have told you before that this love lived until Beatrice's last breath. He mourned her death very deeply. 'Then', he wrote, 'I had an extraordinary vision ... not to ever talk about her again until my words might become worthy of her favour'.

Later, he would write his most beautiful poem and, as I write to you, I think of one of Botticelli's manuscripts about *The Divine Comedy* in parchment, containing one hundred magnificent illustrations, now all at the Berlin Museum, except for six of them which are at the Vatican Apostolic Library. Thirty-four of them were dedicated to *Inferno* alone. In my mind's eye, I can still see one of them, the one that illustrates the eighth song, that of Lucifer. Dante fascinated Botticelli; in fact, the artist painted an extraordinary portrait of him wearing a red cape.

Sandro Botticelli himself had also fallen madly in love, with Simonetta, daughter of the Prince of Florence; it is her face you can see in many of his paintings, such as *Spring*. In our library there is an album I brought from Italy that features Renaissance painters, among which you will find a few of Botticelli's works. Simonetta's face can be spotted immediately in *Birth of Venus*, *Annunciation*, *Fortitude* or *Judith Beheading Holofernes* … Now that I write, I remember that figure with a severed head, just as I remember Herod and Salome with the head of John the Baptist … ah, the beheadings of our times! Surprising a man's attraction to a severed head, to this legend that is resurrected by human society from time to time, to shatter people's lives, their ideals, the utopia of the reshaping of man and the world. Simonetta, just like Beatrice, died young. Forty years later, before his death, Botticelli asked to be buried at the foot of her tomb at the Santa Maria Church in Florence, and not … in the little church called 'Ognissanti' ('All Saints')! … What a great love! Magic. The same as our love, as you to me, the miracle of miracles! Soul of my soul! The shadow of my shadow … All voices and whispers take me to you. And I imagine Florence again and again, because I want to show you the most beautiful paintings in the world, the ones you have not seen, those in the Uffizi or Palazzo Pitti Museum, to show you the art of Botticcelli, Titian, Paolo Uccello … Ah, I imagine that day when we will dip in and get drunk on their paintings and saturate our souls with their colours … We will walk over the old bridge of Arno, over that bridge mapped by Leonardo da Vinci himself …

And you, what are you doing now? Are you asleep or awake? Are you waiting for me, my darling? Are you waiting for me to place my mouth on your mouth, to taste all the world's sweetness?

I am closing this letter here, my darling, as Xhako's brother is waiting to get into the little boat and leave. I have instructed him how to find you.

Your precious Fred …

'*Nil mortalibus ardui est*' … 'Nothing is impossible for humankind'

# THE FOURTH LETTER

> I reached a region silent of all light, which bellows as the sea doth in a storm, if lashed and beaten by opposing winds. The infernal hurricane, which never stops, carries the spirits onward with its sweep, and, as it whirls and smites them, gives them pain.
>
> (Dante, *Inferno* V)

20 July

Dearest Bruna, I write your name and then stop a little as there are a hundred things that I want to tell you all at once. Then, I close my eyes and from that absolute darkness comes a light: the light of you. You arrive just as when you used to hurry towards the house, walking on air, while the wind played with your summer dress. You would run up the stairs two by two, just to fall into my arms and hold me tight. I run like that in my dreams, too, at times – free, searching for you – but I cannot find you, cannot see your eyes, and so I wake up from this nightmare and, unable to fall asleep again, lie down to wait for morning.

At such times, I pick up *Inferno* and start reading some of Dante's work. It is incredible how he imagined Hell's circles to be, the Acheron River and its nine circles. What a genius! When I was a student in Turin, we studied Dante. We studied Dante like we studied Virgil and his *Bucolics*, Petrarch, Boccaccio and the *Decameron*, and lots and lots of other Renaissance authors. And now, as I sit in this monastery corner, I have turned to these works that warm me up like sunbeams. In this place, *Inferno* has another meaning. Every single verse that Dante has written is an excruciating step towards torture and death. I say it is an excruciating step towards death because it makes you aware of who you are; it reminds you, each step of the way, of human strength and its limitations, and defeat and your instinct to survive. Should a man always be strong, stoic? I have seen so many men crying in Tirana, my darling. I do not judge a man who sheds tears, never looked down on any who did …

Dante is no longer the Dante I read years ago; he is now another Dante. The first circle of suffering in *Inferno* consists of religious ignorance. Then come the rest of the circles that condemn those who demanded luxury, the lustful, the greedy ones, the sinners of rage and heresy, the murderers and criminals, the ones who have resisted the Truth and finally those reprobates who have betrayed their neighbour and themselves, turned their backs on the Lord and the Church, the Faith … circles that become wider and wider as they mount to the top. Mighty circles, don't you think?! Everything about Dante makes you reel. *Inferno*, *Purgatory* and *Paradise* … A comedy in three parts, not as people understand 'comedy' here – some show where you go to have a laugh – but the real-life arena where humankind is the main character of its own dramas, comedies or tragedies; a story of death and magical love, just like that of Romeo and Juliet or Tristan and Isolde, Héloise and Abelard – stories of the greatest lovers of this world who continue to be born and to die again and again, generation after generation, century after century.

Tell me, my darling, why does great love often carry with it something tragic, something that smells of blood and ashes! A vicious circle of tragic events that bring terrible soul-searching and then the challenge of self-sacrifice. It all seems as if, finding youself in a burning tree about to be consumed by the flames, you hear onlookers call out: 'Do you dare jump? Are you ready to come face-to-face with your death and to tell us how far you would go for love?' And you know, you know it all too well: I would do that, I would do whatever it takes for you!

With us here is someone called Sotir, a pleasant young man but one who has lost it completely. In fact, he doesn't even understand why he is here. He has periods of clarity now and then, and when this happens you come to understand his beautiful life philosophy. He was the son of one of the members of government during the fascist occupation. He studied theatre in Rome, theatrical direction; the subject of his graduation was one of Pirandello's famous plays, *Non si sa come* [*It Is Not Known How*], but he did not get to defend it because the war started and the borders closed. When he tried to escape to Italy with a small boat from the south, he got caught and was imprisoned immediately. Infuriated after he had exhausted all his pleas for forgiveness, he started screaming and shouting in the courtroom, abusing the prosecutors, resulting in a long sentence. This destroyed his mental health irreparably and so they tossed him here, away from everyone and everything he ever knew. At times, suddenly, he starts reciting Leopardi's poetry or parts of his thesis in Italian. The soldiers can't stand it – to begin with, they laugh at him, then they abuse him, and in the end they kick him hard, taking turns, so painful to watch, until he can no longer move or make a sound.

One day, he assigned roles to all of us, and started declaiming Pirandello's words. It is the story of an unintentional crime, committed in a moment of madness, but the sort of crime that becomes the source of the character's pain and suffering. So much so that, in the end, he turns himself in. He was so excited! He told us that in 1935 this role was assigned to Alexander Moisi by Pirandello himself, as the Italian dramaturg considered him to be one of the best actors in the world, but days before the premiere at the Vienna Theatre, Alexander Moisi died of pneumonia. Sotir also told us that when he chose this piece for his defence, his professor, perplexed, asked him why he had made such a choice. And he had told him that Pirandello expected this drama to be played by a world-class actor of Albanian descent and that, as an Albanian, Sotir wanted to fulfil the dream of the Italian master. In fact, this is such a moving, emotional piece. We did our best to make him feel happy, if even for a little while. He got so excited, he started screaming and then suddenly fell into my lap, crying like a child. I tried to make him feel better and eventually he fell asleep.

One day, my darling, I will tell you about my days under interrogation in Tirana's prison cells. On the other side of the wall was a very well-known writer. I didn't realize at first, but one day he started knocking on the wall with a stone. And so we came up with our communication code where the number of knocks represented a different letter and the length of the pauses between the knocks allowed us to form words. What a place! Late at night, we would hear noises that meant that someone was being taken out, God knows where. Another day, someone jumped from the window of the interrogation room and died instantly. Quite often, we would be woken up by the screaming of men who could no longer stand the torture. It was so frightening. We continued to talk. It lasted three weeks. One morning, I knocked on the wall to ask whether he knew which one of us had been taken the night before, but I didn't get an answer. In the deep silence of my cell, I realized that my dear friend was the one who had been taken God knows where …

More trauma yesterday. Kamberi, the poet, had been missing for two days without a trace. Soldiers searched all over the island. They allowed us to join the search, too, but we could not find him. The alarm went off. The officer who serves on the other side came and checked on us and ordered that we restart the search. Finally, the Bulldog found him hidden in a pit, at the other end of the forest, covered with branches, writing poetry. Poor man, the soldiers brought him into the middle of the monastery and beat him up savagely right in front of us. Bulldog was panting, white foam coming out of his mouth, and kicked him in the face. It seems they broke his jaw, for now Kamberi cannot chew. We feed him only food softened with water. He cannot stand deprivation of liberty … ah, these poets! … Today they brought out a big wild dog and tied him up at the lieutenant's cabin. He bares his teeth at us and growls night and day, and to me, he resembles Cerberus in Dante's *Inferno*, only with a single head!

Since that day, from time to time, in the middle of the night, Bulldog comes through the monastery door with his automatic rifle and searches every corner, in case one of us has yet again disappeared into the forest. Holding a lantern in his hands, he walks in between beds as if he were

Mephistopheles. The light then seems like some kind of projector that smites our frail bodies as they sink to rest, as well as the faces of each of the saints in succession so they, too, seem upset because someone or something is waking them up in the middle of the night. They appear angry but growl *sotto voce*, being unable to roar and bellow. Then Bulldog pulls the monastery door shut and a deadly silence falls upon us all.

I've already hidden away your letters because, occasionally, Bulldog conducts searches and I do not want your letters to be taken away from me. It is midnight and there is an immense silence, as if a holy hand has worked its magic and stopped time, the universe. It is at this moment that I start thinking of you. One night, I dreamed that I flew out of the window and came to you, just like an angel. I floated up in the air, through this dense frost. The clouds pushed me towards you. And you were waiting there, by the window, as if you had known about this heavenly adventure. 'Why so late?', you said. I didn't say a thing, I just took you in my arms, I embraced your legs as if you were a Phidias sculpture, whispering: 'All this longing – I'm burning!' And then I saw lightning rip the sky. Far away, I could hear thunder …

'*Surge et ambula*' … 'Get up and walk'

Yours forever, Fred

* * *

It is well past midnight. Only the sound of the wind striking the large windows and the old wooden door of the monastery can be heard from time to time. Everyone is fast asleep under their grimy covers; someone keeps sleep-talking, two others are snoring heavily.

'Fix the engines!', screams Xhevo.

A laugh or two, the snoring stops and then a long sigh followed by someone else's groan; a constantly pulsating collective pain; body pain, soul pain. Here, you can sense its enormity, slowly swelling against a man's chest until it brings him to his knees, pushing him down until he is unable to stand erect or to hold up his head again, ever. A place where pain is the great dictator ...

The wind keeps blowing. A great silence begins to reign over the thin, rag-clothed bodies, these abandoned subjects of Dante. Confined in this place, they have forgotten how to smile, yet in the world outside, Stalin reigns in people's hearts as 'our father', an icon of the masses. These men, desperate and without a single hope in the world, have plunged into the world of dreams where everything seems once again possible.

Around the walls of the huge dormitory, the apostles seem peaceful, too. Saint Mark, Saint Nicholas, Saint John are observing them. 'Only he who suffers greatly may truly be deserving of the love of God, of the Lord Jesus Christ', they seem to say. And there is Mary, the baby in her arms, casting her tender, compassionate gaze over these condemned people in their profound hibernation.

Who painted these faces? Onufri, Shpataraku, Selenica or some anonymous painter? No one knows. Fred seems to think it is Onufri, the great Albanian exponent of the colour red. He conceived of such a thing because of the luminous rosy glaze that infused the figures of some of the saints. Petro is not convinced. Why Onufri? How did he acquire such a name? The name of a saint. Was it because he wandered long or suffered greatly in search of another world? Onufri, the monk, the ascetic, the hermit who had left the monastery, had walked through the Egyptian desert, stopping at last at a water fountain, with just a raggedy loincloth to cover his nakedness. Perhaps that's why they considered him holy: Saint Onufri!

These poor convicts lying there had nothing in common with the saints looking down on their tired bodies and souls. Their present suffering was too great for words, their future without any hope.

Didn't Dante write: 'Abandon all hope, ye who enter here'?

* * *

# THE FIFTH LETTER

> I then stretched out my hand a little way, and from a sturdy thorn-tree plucked a twig, whereat its trunk cried out: 'Why dost thou rend me?' Then, after growing dark with blood, its cry began again: 'Why dost thou break me off? Hast thou no spirit of compassion in thee? Men were we once, and now are stocks become; thy hand ought surely to have had more pity, even if the souls of serpents we had been.'
>
> (Dante, *Inferno* XIII)

4 August

My sweet darling! For days I was expecting your letter but nothing came and so I got worried that you might have fallen ill again. A thousand things went through my head. But yesterday, the letter finally arrived. You say that you had to sell the red floral dress, the one that I sent you from Italy, so that you could buy some food. Oh how this news has upset me! I feel beyond sad. Did you think that you would never wear it again? But you are wrong, my dear: you would, you would have worn it again. You could have sold my wedding suit, the old wall clock or even the big lamp. Now you have recovered from pneumonia, you need to eat well. That would have raised enough money for food and even for a trip to come and see me in these tough times for you and mother …

These last two or three years have taught me a lot, Bruna. I have learned that endurance and hope are the only way to survive and I will endure all the horrors and catastrophes, I will do it not for myself but for you and mother. I am your husband, I will do everything I can, just to be able to see you again, to have you near, to rest my head on your breast, no matter if I will ever wake up again. It is by rehearsing these thoughts that I pass the time here … We must try to give hope to one another. I read your letter so many times! I know it now by heart.

A few days ago, I walked some way into the forest. It was hot and as I was walking among the cypress trees, I made an interesting discovery: near the small stream, I saw an ants' nest. Hundreds and hundreds of ants went in and out of a tunnel and then disappeared somewhere. They marched under a broken branch, climbing over a little soil mountain and then coming down in perfect order. I lay down on top of dirt and kept watching them intently, as if I were Gulliver. Amazing how organized they are, an extraordinary collective intelligence!

The queen stood in a rather stately way. Most of them were worker ants, among which one group specializes in cutting the leaves; another group transports them to a nest deep underground. Among them are also what are called the soldier ants, those that surge out to catch other insects. Here's what I saw: the queen was surrounded by soldier ants. Soon there came another, perhaps one of those special reconnaissance ones. Surely they were given some sort of signal, because an army of them immediately followed and they fell on top of each other. I followed their moves quietly and came to a place where a great crumpled beetle lay on its back and could not turn. Then the queen ant fast-spun her antennae. Little soldier ants set off toward the beetle and within a minute they covered it almost entirely, turning it into what seemed like a tight ant-ball. They seemed to have finally destroyed it. Then the hauling of the beetle began with extraordinary heft. The queen moved forward, and her army followed her to the nest, pulling along the dead beetle. Funnily enough, this reminded me of the dragging of Mussolini's remains through Milan's Piazzale Loreto square and then the hanging of him by his legs. A kind of giant black beetle!

Anyway, I just wanted to say that the collective life of ants can teach people something about organizational skills, order, solidarity. Is it perhaps that the life of the ants made the famous utopians – Campanella, Thomas More or Erasmus – imagine utopian societies? That evening, it was very windy. I thought about the ants' nest all night long. Did the thunderstorm destroy the nest overnight? In the morning, the sky was blue and I went to look at it again. I found the ants on the move, trying to get around a little channel of draining water in search of food. And so, looking at them intently for a long time, I fell asleep. The soldier's heavy boot woke me up.

My sweet darling! Why did you ask me to stop translating *Inferno* and not look at it again? Are you afraid that someone will find out or are you worried that this will cause me to fall deeper into the sadness and the pain of this world? You reminded me of our happy days, all the crazy things we did together, so that I would forget where I am and leave aside Dante's *Inferno*. You will perhaps be surprised to know that by thinking of it as a literary text, by concentrating on finding the right words in Albanian that match every single word in *Inferno*, I do in fact manage not to think of my own living hell here.

I try really hard to bring the text in Albanian as close to the original as possible, even though it is very hard, as Dante was a word master! He wrote in a three-line rhyme scheme, something totally different from traditional verse, an innovative form for his time. He often uses mystical words with dual meanings that are very hard to decipher and translate well into another language. I also need to find the equivalent slang words that I have not used before. Sometimes I ask my friends here and they help me a lot, because they come from different parts of the country and so make the language I use colourful.

But more importantly, I am preoccupied with preserving Dante's poetic form and style. Again, when the night falls, with my eyes transfixed on the monastery's ceiling, I see my friends' bodies lying in pain, tossing and turning, trying to find a moment of peace. Sotir talks in his sleep and the old man prays to die as soon as possible; Sazan chokes coughing and you fear that any moment now he will take his last breath and give in to the eternal silence.

It is then that I start thinking of Dante's *Inferno* all over again – I start living it; I enter into dark, deep, damp labyrinths and find it impossible to get out. I scream in my head; I want to punch the sky, but no one, no one can hear me. My voice is lost in the silence of the night. Desperation. What a world! I think of Homer, of the King of Hades, the Greek Hell of mythology; I imagine Erebus with its three proximal palaces: the 'Night Palace', 'The Palace of Dreams' and the 'Palace of Sleep' in a place of dark, thick and frightening fog. I remember when I taught my students about Homer and Tartarus, the vilest pit of Hell, where criminals were punished, the place where they drove Sisyphus himself, the dungeons of those overthrown and defeated by the Olympian lords, giants and Titans. Acheron, the son of the Sun and Moon, was condemned and turned into a dark, deep river just for giving water to the Titans. The place where Charon would take you in his boat, a place of no return.

Yet – some did, some did return, Bruna. Will we be back? … Oh darling, let's not be sad, because dreams are the last thing left to us in this life. Speaking of dreams: one night, I was having a nightmare where I was writhing at the thought of dying in that dark and cold river. I dived in a couple of times and nearly drowned but suddenly, a strong hand caught me by my hair, pulled me out and threw me into a small boat. I thought of Charon, but of course it was Rrapush, our own little Charon, Zaratha's kind old man.

I got the photos you sent to me, my darling! What a thrill! A photo is more precious than the daily bread in here. I now keep it with me all the time; it is always there, in the inner pocket of my old jacket, next to my heart.

When I sit alone on the shore, I take it out and start talking to you … I lose myself in your eyes … I look away, towards the top of the first roofs of the village, and I am reminded of our home, our free life, our love, everything … I see the Gjuhadoli Road gleaming with rime and fog, an image that, after a few minutes, comes vividly to life. My heart beats faster, I feel elated, filled with excitement. Though in a world of loneliness, I always recall the day I saw you for the first time. You were with a group of friends … remember? It was a Sunday, Shkodra had just been liberated and the streets were flooded with happiness. Suddenly you sensed my gaze and you told your friends; instantly they turned their heads. I continued to smile in your direction and they realized it was the sweet look of love. For a moment there, I felt awkward and wanted to turn back and run. But I froze in front of you, facing you, I kept gazing, not yet knowing that you would be the love of my life!

Give my poor mother a big kiss from me, Bruna. Please love her, love her for me and you. Since the passing of my father, I have been the only joy in her life. I hold you tight, my darling, in my heart, sweetheart!

Fred, from the other world …

'*Ita diis placuit*' … 'The gods will have it so'

# THE SIXTH LETTER

> Charon, the demon, with his ember eyes makes beckoning signs to them, collects them all, and with his oar beats whoso takes his ease. Even as in autumn leaves detach themselves, now one and now another, till their branch sees all its stripped off clothing on the ground; so, one by one, the evil seed of Adam cast themselves down that river-bank at signals, as doth a bird to its recalling lure. Thus, o'er the dusky waves they wend their way; and ere they land upon the other side, another crowd collects again on this.
>
> (Dante, *Inferno* III)

10 August

This morning as I sat near the lagoon, I heard music. I was truly surprised: music that came from afar. Music on this island isolated from the rest of the world, abandoned by all the angels. But little by little, the sound was becoming clearer; I started hearing a tango we once danced together in the city park where the old band played for their own pleasure, and ours of course. Do you remember? Ah that New Year's Eve I was really happy, totally drunk! For a few moments we stopped to listen to the midnight sound of the old cathedral bells. The old band continued to play and we danced, we danced drunk with each other. You would turn and turn, laughing as if you were weightless and I continued to hold you in my arms as if you were my child, my little baby. One moment I held your delicate hand and kissed your lovely fingers and then your shoulders, I felt your skin getting warmer, your cheeks getting hot and felt your desire for us to be alone, somewhere else, in our world of desire and ecstasy. Oh how I would love to turn back the clock and live in that moment just one more time and then I could die happy. What really constitutes happiness if not a few unforgotten moments that become the entire meaning of this life? As I write, darling, I dance with you and I want you to believe that. I hold you in my arms, I lift you up on my fingertips as if you were the most beautiful butterfly in the world. You are everything to me; you are me, I am you. You are all I've got in this crushing loneliness.

They look down on us here all the time, we are humiliated daily but I feel different, I feel proud that you are my love, happy that I live all my dreams with you, in the roads we have travelled and we will be travelling together in days to come. I obliterate all this miserable life in here with your image, your eyes that follow me constantly, and your beautiful body made of flesh, honey and blood. Here, right behind the monastery, a plum tree has sprung up. It has grown just like that, in the middle of nowhere, at a place where only small plants straggle forth, plants where wild rabbits hide. One day, I removed all the suffocating weeds around the little tree so that it could breathe easier. I dug the soil and made a little canal bordered by pebbles, so that when it rains, the water can travel towards the roots. It won't be long before it blooms, bringing a little joy into this dark and sad place.

You wrote that Lazer was impressed with the quality of the translation of *Paradise* and that he has now finished reading the few first parts of the *Inferno*. So he thinks that it is a good quality translation overall, then? This has made me really happy. I am even happier with the fact that he is now typing it all, something which I would never have been able to do in these conditions. Be good to Lazer, Bruna; he is like a brother to me. I am aware of his family's ties with the local politicians but Lazer is a close friend to me and he will always be loyal and good to me; it is a friendship that no ideology can destroy. Remember that …

Here everything is the same; the only news we get is a word here and there from Rrapush. He goes to Vlora from time to time and brings to us whatever he hears on his little trips about what happens in the world. It is true and absolutely a good thing that the farmers have claimed their land, that a lot of schools have reopened their doors so that our children can learn to read and write, that factories can secure enough goods to make up for all the destruction that war brought upon us. But it is equally important to allow for a healthy opposition, to stop punishing and imprisoning anyone who opposes the regime, depriving them of their freedom, taking from them by force everything they have ever worked for. I hope that now the political spying campaign finally winds up, and people are able to get on with their lives in peace.

My lovely Bruna, sweetheart, I hope that by now you are used to working in the flour factory. I know that it is way too far from the house so I wanted to remind you that in the cellar, there is an old 'Bianchi' bicycle; I brought it with me when I came back from Italy. Fix it and use it to get to and from work. This way you won't have to walk for an hour back and forth every day.

I try to picture you working, my darling, your hands covered in that flour, your whitened hands … and when I eat bread here, I imagine it is the bread made with the flour that your hands touch every day. Though our bread is dark, dry and stale. And then I can evoke the smell of your body, the scent of your breasts and I feel so sad, so desperate that I didn't make you happy enough, I didn't plant the seed of our own fruit in your beautiful body. You used to always tell me that we have plenty of time, you wanted to wait to finish renovating the house, but time was deceitful, it lied to us, it separated us: we never imagined our time would turn out this way.

As I write to you now, I am sitting near the church, beside 'the circle' as they call it – a slab of stone – where, they say, people come from everywhere to find healing. It certainly has something to do with the fact that people believe it to be a magic, mystical place where miracles happen. For centuries, those who are sick in mind and body have been coming here for resolution to their problems. Me too, right now, I am sitting and praying at this place where miracles are supposed to take place. But you know, miracles do not come to my suffering friends and me; the only thing that blooms is the hope I keep alive inside of me. This hope has the colour of your eyes …

Fred, dreaming of you

*'Agnosco veteris vestigia flammae'* … 'I see in you traces of the ancient flame'

* * *

For months, Dante's shadow did not cease following Fred: Dante with his long coat and eyes like balls of fire that light up the darkness. At night, whenever the door made that creaking noise, Xhevo or Kamberi would turn to Fred, translating still under candlelight, whispering to him:

'Hey, Freddo, get up … someone is looking for you!'

'Who is it?'

'Dante, you moron, who else! …'

And then everyone would laugh, Fred too.

'Naughty boys! …'

One morning, they all woke up to an unusually dark sky.

'Black clouds are approaching!', cried Sotir.

'No, they are not clouds', said Sazan. 'That's smoke released by the Russian Navy leaving the naval base.'

For a moment everyone went quiet, then:

'The Westerners are coming!', exclaimed Kamberi.

Fred shook his head, no.

'For the sake of Stalin's moustache, Albania will end up alone, abandoned by all.'

The day after, on the opposite shore, a group of soldiers was seen installing a large cannon facing the sea.

Leaving his post and turning towards the convicts, Bulldog started striding back and forth, yelling: 'Bravo! … No one can defeat Albania now! Our enemies will end up shoved in the bore of this cannon … Long live Father Stalin!'

And he waved his Kalashnikov over his head.

'And what do you think you're doing standing all bunched up there … go on, scram! Disappear!'

The crowd of prisoners looked at him silently as the soldiers started raising the muzzle of the cannon as if about to aim at someone, or something.

* * *

# THE SEVENTH LETTER

> 'Let us go on, for it is willed in Heaven that I should show another this wild road.'
>
> (Dante, *Inferno* XXI)

25 August

Dearest Bruna, ten days ago it was the feast of the Assumption of our Most Holy Lady. I have written to you already about this gorgeous fresco, *The Assumption of the Virgin Mary*, painted on the walls of the old church by an anonymous Albanian artist around the seventeenth century.

That morning, when we walked out of the monastery, we saw a group of villagers arguing with the officer. He had another three guards behind him, clutching automatic rifles. We could also see the silhouette of the priest in his long black cloak, disappearing towards the little boat. The officer went inside the improvised cabin and came out again. It appeared that the priest had spoken to the authorities and, in the end, a little concession had been made for this special day.

Rrapush dropped the priest and three other villagers over on our side of the island and returned to pick up the rest of the people waiting for him. The red flag was just being raised by one of the guards, a sign to let the men in, when the officer screamed: 'Where is your permission? Let me see it.' 'We left it with the other officer', replied the priest. 'This is a strategic zone! No civilian visitors or priests allowed!', he yelled.

But the priest did not falter! He shot him a dirty look and, unafraid, continued towards the church. The lieutenant made no move. When he got near us, the priest made a sign telling us to follow him. We started walking but it didn't take long before we heard the officer's voice: 'Stop! You have nothing to do with the church; you are prisoners!' We had to stop at once. The priest and the three villagers pushed the heavy door open and slipped into the church. I stood a little closer to the door, making sure that the officer did not notice. The priest lit the candles one by one, and the incense, ready to start the Mass. Four other villagers walked in and Rrapush left to bring more people still. There were well over fifteen in the church when the priest started the service. We could hear them sing psalms dedicated to the Virgin Mary. The priest, too, started singing in his beautiful baritone: 'I praise you because I am fearfully and wonderfully made; your works are wonderful. I know that full well.'

On the thick church walls, the frescos were shining like never before; the sun streamed through the glass windows, caressing the beautiful faces of the saints. At the end of the ceremony, the priest left the church to visit the cemetery. He spent a few minutes in silence contemplating the resting place of his predecessor and then returned with all the other people to the little boat. Rrapush was exhausted, but happy to have been of service on such a rare occasion. By lunchtime, the heat had become unbearable and so we went indoors to the cool, where I continued to translate *Inferno.*

My dearest, I would prefer not to tell you what I am about to write because I know that this will cause you much sadness, but I cannot keep it all to myself. I must tell someone: Stavri is living out his last days. He is not well at all. Last night he asked me to sit close to him and he whispered: 'I want to ask you a big favour: to be near me when I die, to make sure my eyes are closed and to tie this ribbon around my neck. It is the only thing I have left from my wife.' It broke my heart. Death in this place is really affecting us all. And then he cried. He handed me an old wallet and told me that there were some photos of his wife and children in it. 'I don't want them to go missing', he said. Tears of pain and longing, Bruna. He has been here for a very long time. Two war wounds tell the story of his character, of who he is. He is one of the very first communists; he had a lot of dreams. He fought for a new Albania, a nation united, an ideal communism.

At the beginning, when I heard that he was such a committed communist, I gave him the cold shoulder, but soon I realized what he was made of and what a good man he was. He was such an idealist! He spoke often of communism and Karl Marx. He condemned Stalinism, which he called 'the progeny of great evil' because they were the first to start the political processes that involved the opposition's disappearance, and the cult of the leader. Stavri possessed vast knowledge about the great utopians, Thomas More and Campanella. He worshipped Erasmus, that great and free citizen of Europe. So, gradually, Stavri became very dear to me.

He spoke softly, harbouring no hatred, even though he had been robbed of his freedom for such a long time. He saw the world differently, he saw the future of Albania differently. Stavri's world was beautiful. Although excluded from his party, he was proud to call himself a communist. 'I'm one of the real ones', he would often tell me. 'They have no idea what Marxism is … these are Stalinists, people of violence.' He spoke of freedom and democracy, something we all want, and he knew all the leaders of today. I was surprised and one day I came to the realization: 'I am like him, I think like him'. Stavri talked about the future, our youth, education, the drive for a new culture and mindset. He talked about Socrates, Plato and the great Greeks; the tragedians, especially Sophocles, whose theatre he loved very much, because those tragedies have shaken humanity down the ages. He talked to me about the Greek *demos*. When he was young, he travelled to Greece and was inspired by their ancient culture to see the world through a different lens. 'We are like the dove's wings', he said to me once. 'A one-winged dove cannot fly. We must unite our ideals for this land, this country of ours that is so thirsty and hungry.'

In the first few months here, I often asked Petro what time it was. He would pull his old watch out of his vest's little pocket, open the lid, look at it, and laugh at me, saying, 'Twelve' or 'Whatever o'clock', adding: 'Why do you need the time, my friend?' or 'Can we stop Our Time? Tell me!' It was a beautiful watch he had bought in Detroit, when he was living there as an immigrant. One night he told us about his trip to America – what a voyage, sailing to the USA from Le Havre in France! On the way to the Caribbean, they encountered a terrible storm. The water flooded the deck in no time and they would all have drowned, but luckily the storm blew over and they all made it to shore. Petro himself had jumped into the churning waters and saved the life of an American who was drowning, the very same man who later took him in and gave him a job at his factory. He regarded Petro as a son, and even wanted him to marry his daughter and inherit all he owned. But Petro kept thinking of his village, his pregnant wife who by then had given birth to a little girl. Ten years later, heartbroken because he was very fond of the American girl, he returned to Albania. His family was waiting for him and he knew that the whole time. He returned to Albania the same year the country was occupied by the Germans!

Bruna, darling, I just finished translating the nineteenth song. It was an arduous task, but I managed it. I also got tired trying to economize. I am running out of paper and, to save it, I am compelled to write in tiny letters. So much so that sometimes I cannot even read my own Albanian writing, I cannot distinguish the words I have chosen to render the original. But of course, what really overwhelms me is Dante's thoughts and impressions, the analogy of it all with the life I live here. So, I take a break to get rid of all my bad thoughts, since they frustrate and sadden me, causing me to lose the thread of translation. So, it is during these moments that I think of you, I leave the world I am in, I fly to the heavens and come to you, my love, my sweetheart, I skim back and forth, reliving those moments that are eternally imprinted in my head and my vision. Remember how we kissed and laughed while passing a cherry into one another's mouths? I would start by placing a cherry between my lips and then you would take it with yours and I would do the same, take it from yours to mine until the smooth skin of the fruit would break and the sweet juice would turn our lips into a translucent red and we would kiss …

Loads of kisses, my dearest,

Fred

'*Vide cor tuum!*' … 'Look into your heart!'

# THE EIGHTH LETTER

> 'When in the sweet ray's presence thou shalt be of Her whose lovely eyes see everything, from her thou'lt know the journey of thy life.'
>
> (Dante, *Inferno* X)

15 September

Dearest Bruna, I am writing this letter again, just as I wrote to you yesterday morning, as everything that I write is imprinted on my memory, every word, every breath I take while I write to you, every bit of pain I experience. Yesterday was a beautiful, warm sunny day, and I was leaning against the wall of the silent church, those smooth stones that who knows how many hands, hundreds and thousands of hands have touched, believing that a miracle could be possible. Is it possible? Could a miracle happen? I am one of these people who hopes for such a miracle to happen ... And so, I was thinking of such possibility and writing when Bulldog slowly edged close to me – like a black shadow, like an animal that jumps over its prey – and snatched the paper from my hands. 'What is this?', he asked. 'A letter', I answered quietly. 'A letter? ... Hmm! To whom?' 'To my family.' Meanwhile, grinding his teeth, he drew his eyes even closer to the letter to be able to read my small writing. 'Badmouthing the government, huh?! The government that handed land to the poor! Or the government that took the hidden gold from you! Well, we did it! ...' 'What gold?', I said.

'We live such simple lives … I'm a teacher, sir!' 'Do not call me "sir"!', he exclaimed, 'not even a comrade, because you cannot be my comrade. I am your enemy!' … And he began to tear the letter into small pieces. It pierced my heart, even though I had written that letter into my soul beforehand. Nothing could be achieved by tearing up that letter, not a single word could be erased! Yes, sweetheart. Even in my sleep, at night, my thoughts are with you, I have you with me, sitting on my eyelids.

Darling, last night I started to work on the sixth song. It is the song in which Dante describes the third circle of Hell. I translated until midnight under the light of a burning pine tree branch, because after dark, the lights go off here. The scene where a three-headed dog, Cerberus, which keeps an eye out so that no one passes through, is a horrible and scary scene … 'The circle with an everlasting rain', Dante writes, where it is damn cold and it always hails, it snows; a ruthless atmosphere, where Cerberus, the guardian, tears souls and humans apart. It reminded me of one of our old tales, published some ten years ago in the Nation's Depository, along with some old anecdotes and old Albanian legends. It reminded me of the monsters, the quads, those supernatural beings which guarded the entrance to the afterlife, the Underground, the world where the dead lived, or the so-called 'eternally condemned', because they had not obeyed the deities … At the very start, Dante wrote his favourite phrase: 'Abandon all hope, ye who enter here'. Can hope be lost? I do not want to lose it, but there are moments when hope leaves me, as if it drugs my soul away and I feel as if my chest were all empty, there is no sound, no air … 'Abandon all hope, ye who enter here.' They were words written on a door, in a dark colour, Dante wrote. He tells the man who accompanies him: 'Master, do you hear? Who are the people who resemble the shattered from sufferings?'

Bruna, the more I work on *Inferno*, the more I am astonished at the immensity of Dante's imagination. The giant, multi-dimensional scenes engulf an entire human world, get to the essence of what it is to be a human being. Dante was extraordinary. You know, I read many early authors since I studied Latin, but no one comes near Dante. Certainly, there is Virgil with his great lyricism, with his famous *Bucolics*, Dante's guide through

Inferno and Purgatory, but it is Dante who shakes you up, makes you think, philosophize – he makes you pay attention to everything around you. Imagine a Dante who spent most of his life on the roads of Italy, in exile, persecuted and sentenced to death. He never returned to Florence but remained on the roads like a Jew, always searching for his homeland. Art, literature, humanism became Dante's true motherland.

When I finished half the song, my eyes were tired, my eyelids shut, but I could not sleep because that terrible creature kept on following me, turning sometimes into the face of my moustache-bearing investigator, who only knew one thing: how to torture me, how to hang me upside down, so that I would admit to things I hadn't done, which would supposedly ease my punishment. O Lord! What a nightmare! What we wanted to establish was a social-democratic party, but this government wants only one party, its own – a party of a single man or of a handful of people hungry for power. Two days ago, I learned that Father Fishta's bones have been thrown into the river. Can it be true? Can we really sink so low as to throw away the bones of one of the greatest Albanians who has ever lived? Is admitting to becoming a member of Mussolini's Italian Academy a good enough reason? … In the investigator's room, they reminded me of our friendship and my friendship with Father Anton Harapi. What could I say except the truth, that the good soul was totally committed to the Holy See? And so, they returned me to my cell but his face would not leave the room until the morning; it would turn into Cerberus's face – something that happened again last night.

When they took me to the investigator's room, they told me that I was an activist of the Dante Alighieri Association and that this association was led by Peteci, a fascist … and that I was aware of it. I admitted I have lectured on Dante, *The Decameron*, Petrarch, Pirandello and D'Annunzio, but this was not related at all to fascism, because when we met, we also spoke about Leonardo da Vinci, Michelangelo, the Sistine Chapel … To talk about Dante does not mean to glorify or sing hymns to fascism. If I have spoken of the standard-bearers of Italian literature, as did Lazer Shantoja who translated *Faust* written by Goethe, I did it because they are the representatives and forerunners of a new civilization. No one can deny or dismiss their work … And so, my darling, I tried so hard to get rid of his terrible face, the Cerberus-like face of the man who investigated me. I then got up and went out to look at the stars. I looked up and started my heavenly journey towards you. I flew close to the Milky Way looking for you!

My lovely Bruna! You always tell me that you are strong and that you are enduring all the weight of the great pain our separation inflicts on you. Is it true that everything is going well? Has the chest pain that stopped you from breathing really gone away? From what I read, it seems my mother has now accepted my fate. Let's hope! What about your mother, how is she doing? and your father? The cherry tree in the backyard has long shed its last fruit, and yet I still see its green branches and leaves playing up in the air. Do you remember when I fell asleep under that cherry tree? I was resting my head on your lap. I had just finished fixing the roof and I was exhausted when you started singing a love song. Your sweet voice put me to sleep as if I were a child. Remind me of the song, won't you? I seem to have forgotten which one it was. In your last letter, you mention that you now go to work by bike. This has made me very happy as you won't have to walk all the way to the factory, back and forth every day. I imagine you on the bicycle, by the lake, with the wind from the village of Shiroka playing on your cotton summer dress, and this makes me forget where I am. I see my Beatrice, my divine woman. I have opened my arms, my beloved, hugging you as you move through the wind, in this beautiful rapture of nature.

Fred …

'*Amor vincit omnia*' … 'Love conquers all'

# THE NINTH LETTER

> I turned, and at my side I looked, afraid of having been abandoned, when I saw the ground was dark in front of me alone. When wholly turned, my Comforter began: 'Why still distrustful? Dost thou not believe that I am with thee, and am guiding thee?'
>
> (Dante, *Purgatory* III)

2 October

My Beatrice … today I am calling you by the name of Dante's great love. Yesterday was 1 October and the wind stopped as if by magic. The sky opened up, and the clouds scattered at a strange speed, as if being pushed by a magical, divine hand. I was sitting there all sad at the monastery's doorstep when I saw a silhouette approaching the guard on the other side. It was a woman.

At first, I thought that it might be you, hoping that with the help of Lazer's friends you might have secured a 'permission to visit'; then I noticed the woman's long hair and I realized that it was Stavri's wife. She spoke to the guard and waited on the shore for a while until Rrapush arrived and got on to the little boat, heading towards the island. My heart started pounding and I quickly ran inside to let others know that she had arrived. Within ten minutes, she was standing at the door.

We had formed two rows on either side but stood silent, not knowing what to say. Zel, Stavri's wife, was carrying a big bag, probably loaded with food. I had chills all over. My whole body was shaking. She was trying really hard to spot her husband among us and stood there surprised at her failure to do so. She looked at us with frightened eyes, while the lieutenant read the 'permission to visit' letter, muttering through his teeth. No one could hear what he was saying …

Rrapush greeted the lieutenant, lifted his right hand in a kind hello to us, and as he turned away promised the woman, 'I'll be back to pick you up in two hours!' The lieutenant quickly intervened and said loudly, 'No, Rrapush, wait – wait here for her, she will be going back with you right away!' Surprised, Rrapush made a sign as if to say: What are you talking about, she just arrived! 'Now? What do you mean, why?', he asked. Meanwhile Sefer and Xhako took a step closer to Zel. We all followed suit. Zel sensed something bad had happened. We all lined up and hugged her, one by one. 'Tell me, what has happened to him? Have they taken him somewhere else? Maybe he has fallen ill and is lying in a bed someplace else?'

We accompanied her to the entrance of the big hall, where she stopped, afraid of going any further. She looked at Stavri's empty bed and screamed! She had hoped to see him at least lying there, in his bed on the floor, just one more time. 'Where is he, tell me? Why the hell are you standing there and looking at me like this?' Faced with silence, she moved close to me and, with the saddest and most pleading eyes I have ever seen, demanded: 'At least you, tell me!' I gave her a hug and whispered: 'Didn't they notify you? … Stavri left us, two nights ago. He now rests in peace …" But she screamed with the loudest voice, turning to face the wall of the saints. She gazed at them and sobbed, firing a barrage of questions. It seemed crazy, if she was looking for Stavri among the saints' faces. Our poor Stavri! My heart had sunk; I felt so powerless, I couldn't do anything for this poor woman. Xhako and I held her as we walked her towards the door. She remembered her bag and stopped for a moment, picked it up and put it in our hands. 'Here, take it; it is for you. You were his brothers', she murmured, now completely cold and shattered. At the monastery's doorstep, she asked to be taken to his grave, in the corner of the cemetery, right beside the monks' graves. When we got there nearly, she threw herself on the fresh mound with its wooden cross and almost passed out. Dissolved in tears. Zel remained lying there with all that remained of her dear husband, for a long time. She cried and cried, all the time trying to fix the grave. Her nails and hands became encrusted with dirt.

Dearest Bruna! It was a horrible scene and I cannot go on describing it because my heart hurts. After that, we returned. I put all his belongings in an old bag: his beloved books, a translated book of Victor Hugo, Tolstoy's *War and Peace* in French, as well as *Poor Folk* by Dostoyevsky, a book which I read again here. He lived within the era of the French Revolution. 'It was a Revolution that devoured its own children', he told us, then went on and on about the great friendship and common struggle of Danton and Robespierre, the collapse of the monarchy, the creation of the Republic, how Robespierre decapitated Danton and how the partisan crew of Danton took Robespierre to the guillotine. And it all happened because of Robespierre's own strategy: revolutionary terror!

Zel took his books without saying a word. She also took the letter I wrote to you … Then she gave us all a hug in silence. It was very hard for her to remain standing. She greeted the lieutenant, who stood at the door as if frozen, not knowing what to say, and he took her to the boat where Rrapush was waiting for her. He helped her to jump in and left almost immediately. She didn't take her eyes off us, immobilized, in pain, as if she would never see us again. And she wouldn't …

Finally, the boat arrived at the far bank. After a word to the soldier again on the shore, the little figure became smaller and smaller, climbing the path and disappearing up into the village. The sun was pale that day; no warmth at all came from it. A very cold, mournful day. I kept an apple from those that Zel left for us. At dawn, while still asleep, I could smell apple close to me. I'd forgotten that I hadn't eaten mine as I'd hidden it under that miserable pillow. It was a present from Stavri and I cried.

It was the first time I cried. I thought of his death. Stavri will no longer hear the birds singing in the morning at the monastery grille window. He fed them breadcrumbs there and they were used to it, they had come to expect it … They knew this man loved them. Stavri treated them like his children, but now he is gone and the birds will look for him. Perhaps they will eventually understand that he is gone, that he is no longer among the living. I will do my best to replace him. And so I ask, my dear: how does one define the death of a convict? I believe it should be seen as a double death, don't you think? Stavri will not hear the birds' choir any more, he will not hear their spring concert again. I cried and remembered Mozart's *Requiem* … the very same requiem we heard together at Shkodra's Cathedral. The music plumbed the depths of my soul and it seemed to me that that tremulous song lifted Stavri from his grave, in his prison clothes, all stretched out, lying there, on a sunny day. How terrible the death sentence for a man like him! But do not be sad, my sweet. That day Petro said to me, 'Cry my friend, only the dead do not weep!'

One evening, late, we were about to go to bed when we heard noises coming from the far corner of the monastery. It was Kamberi, crying and talking in his sleep. We rushed to his side to find him with a screwdriver that had gone through his belly button; his hands and bed were drenched in blood. 'I want to die!', he said. 'I want to die! They stole and killed my youth! … They took my life away!' He yelled so loud that the soldiers could hear. We removed the screwdriver, tidied up the wound, put a clean t-shirt on top of it and pressed hard on it to stop the blood coming out, and put him on the straw bed. Sazan stayed with him, trying to calm him down. It took quite some time for him to sleep.

This saddened everyone. I tried hard to fall asleep, but it was impossible after what I had seen. In my head, for one reason or another, I kept seeing images of Dostoyevsky's book *The House of the Dead*. We have this book at home, in Italian. O Lord! I imagined poor Dostoyevsky in forced labour camps in Siberia – there, between the sludge and the crime, the murderers. Despite everything, there was something so inhuman in what they did to those people – great violence, deep contempt, cruelty, as their lives gradually crumbled and were finally lost. Here it is somewhat different though, regardless how much they hate us 'enemies of the people'. But which people? The people, our neighbours, the inhabitants of the city who know us so well, who know who we are? No, it is not the people who despise us. The most revolting thing here is the fact that they bury the dead within the prison grounds and do not release the bodies back to the families, nor do they allow the loved ones to mourn their dead, to see them one last time. Who grants these people the right to do this? Can a dead person be kept a prisoner? This is crazy!

I will leave this letter here, my darling, as everything saddens me now. The fact that you are so far away, even though you rest deep in my heart. I place my lips firmly on yours, kissing you again and again, sweetheart, from far away, away from this world of mourning …

Fred …

'*Gloria victis*' … 'Glory to the vanquished'

* * *

Splish-splash …

Out here, you can get 'star-drunk' if you keep gazing at a bunch of stars for a long time.

Here, if you want, you can extend your arm and touch the moon that has spilt over the waters of the lagoon.

Splish-splash … The old man paddles away and the boat floats over water embroidered by thousands of golden stars.

He avoids looking at the woman with her husband's death in her eyes. Her facial expression set in stone.

A night bird's song explores the air and darkness of the night.

The woman remains silent, quietly sobbing under her breath. The old man can hear the shuddering sounds, but doesn't dare look at her.

Splish-splash … Rrapush keeps paddling away and, for a moment, he feels as if it is not the woman he is taking across the waters on to the shore but her husband locked in his coffin. One more for the other world. 'O Lord, have mercy', Rrapush murmurs and paddles faster.

Splish-splash … the boat glides, and the old man is like Charon of Hades, taking the dead over the waters of the Styx to the empire of death.

Splish-splash …The floodlight from the guards' post on the other side is on, shining brightly by turns on this condemned island, the waters, the boat, Rrapush and the woman who sits there like a statue.

Finally the boat touches the shore and the poor woman hands a shawl to the old Charon. One must give something to the ferryman who transports us to another world …

* * *

# THE TENTH LETTER

> More than a thousand o'er the gates I saw of those that from the heavens had rained, who, vexed, were saying: 'Who is he, that, without death, is going through the kingdom of the dead?'
>
> (Dante, *Inferno* VIII)

4 December

Darling Bruna, our dog Guli passed away. For one last time he looked at me, his eyes glassy. I saw my reflection in those eyes: a bearded, unshaven, very sad man! It was a slow death, during which he moaned as if in great pain, as if he knew he had reached the end. He lay on my feet – his favourite place – as he took his last breath. Whenever it was cold outside, Guli would enter the monastery and stand at my feet to borrow some warmth. Often, shivering, especially at midnight, he would come so close to me that I could feel the beating of his heart. Guli did not know in what times he was living.

I am pretty sure Guli had a soul though. I am convinced that he felt our infinite sadness. When someone came to visit and brought something to eat, Guli had a party because he had a share of everything, like all of us. Guli was everyone's pet. One day Petro put his hat over Guli's head and taught him to lift up his front paws and walk like a circus dog. What a spectacle! We forgot everything that day. He even played postman! We would put things in his mouth to take to the shore, or to someone waiting in the forest. He carried everything between his teeth. We composed a song for Guli and he was probably totally bemused when we sang to him, but he did feel and understand human love. Sometimes he would swim to the shore and go to the village and would return from the village after two or three days, all bright and happy. Once, he returned with another dog, his little girlfriend it appears. They roamed around the island together and rejoiced all day! 'Come on, Guli … ah Guli, you devil!' … Guli had fallen in love. And his little friend would roll around, licking him, sticking her head underneath his chin and rubbing her body against Guli's body. 'Where have you been till now, Guli?', Xhevo would laugh. 'We had no idea you could be such a playful companion!' And we would all crack up, forgetting where we were, forgetting we were in gaol. We forgot our wounds, our sorrows, our lack of freedom. But nothing got past Bulldog. One day he spotted the other dog, and he hurled stones at her, wounding her, and then he threw her into the sea. We never saw the other dog again.

Dearest, yesterday someone arrived here from Tirana, wearing a big black, long coat. His rather unpleasant face was constantly turned towards me. He reminded me of the time of the investigation, when they would wake me up in the middle of the night to ask me all sorts of absurd questions. The visitor took me aside and asked me how I knew Beso, my high school student who helped me to come here, a somewhat privileged place compared to the other terrible prisons. He noticed all too quickly the state I was in after the investigation, as my arm was still in a sling and I couldn't use it to do much at all. I told him that Beso was my student and one of the best in the school, a patriot who dropped out of school when he went to fight in the mountains. He also knew that I had made an appeal, seeking the truth about why I have been incarcerated. But he didn't let much slip regarding this. He asked me about what I had done in Turin at the time Albania was invaded by fascism. I told him that I studied … literature; what else could I have said? I hope that I am wrong, but I was under the impression that something has happened to Beso. Then he went to speak to the lieutenant while continuing to glance at me. He was terrifying. All that afternoon I thought of the high school, the college, the yard where the students would gather, the last photo I took with them during Independence Day celebrations; the Dante Alighieri Association, the screenings of Italian movies and our readings of Pirandello, Leopardi and the other great poets. I get a little teary when I think about all this. Most of my students were fortunate enough to return from the war, I think. One day, in the centre of town, while walking on the 'High Street', I saw a woman in black who was watching me attentively. I slowed down, and she caught up and stood in front of me. I did not immediately recognize her but soon my memory kicked in and I realized that it was Hana, Kujtim's mother. 'Why in black', I said, 'and what happened?' 'Do you not know?', she asked. 'Kujtim was killed in the war!' 'Ah', I whispered and gave her a big bear hug. I felt very sorry. Kujtim was a gentle boy with a wonderful heart who loved literature, wrote incredibly romantic poetry; Migjeni was his idol! He had begun to write in free verse, which as you know I like a lot … Here is a young poet dying on the verge of liberation, I thought. What is a poet's death like? Later, I asked one of my students about the circumstances of Kujtim's death. He told me that he was killed in the mountains of Mirdita, a few days before the liberation of Albania … in one of his pockets they had found a bundle of letters – it was poetry. So, I got my answer, my dear: yes, a poet can die but his songs remain. Interestingly, one of the poems was dedicated to one of his killed friends. Ah, so many unnecessary deaths! …

At sunset, as usual, we all gathered outside the monastery for the evening count, but Xhevo did not come out. Bulldog called out his name, and when he got no answer, he yelled it out at the top of his lungs. Xhevo came out in a hurry and lined up beside me. The lieutenant read his name again, but suddenly a laugh broke out. The first to start laughing in fact was the lieutenant, who was watching us from afar, then it spread to us. Bulldog at first became furious with this laughter, but when he saw Xhevo, he also barked out a laugh and then couldn't stop. Laughter caught us all, even Xhevo himself. Poor man, while rushing to come out, his pants had fallen. He looked ridiculous in his underwear! He quickly pulled them up, but by then we were hysterical. O Lord, we couldn't stop laughing. Prisoners and guards laughing together, indiscriminately. We went to sleep laughing that night. In the dark, as we were trying to fall asleep, Skender called out once again: 'Xhevo, look out for your pants!' We laughed again one last time. It was both absurd and so human at the same time.

Bruna, in your last letter you told me that you had cleaned the whole house and put the sheets out in the sun. And I try to imagine you and your sweetness among these sheets playing with the breeze in the sun, those sheets that are waiting for our bodies to rest on them. Yes, for us to rest in the sweet sleep of love, my dear. To finally rest in the sweet sleep of love. You also tell me that you cleaned and folded all our clothes, including that grey suit of mine that you like so much. How sweet of you to place your dress next to it, facing my suit, so close together, just like your soul and mine are together, always. You tell me that the house smells of jasmine. That makes me so happy! Keep me close, my darling, close enough to smell my body and I yours. You must know, my love, that everything is relative in this life: yes, to be in this Dante-esque place and yet feel happy at the same time. It is paradoxical, but human happiness lies always within the soul …

I hug you ever so tightly, sweetheart, and ask that you do not worry about me.

Your Fred … yours always!

'*Sursum corda*' … 'Lift up your hearts'

# THE ELEVENTH LETTER

> 'Therefore get up! O'ercome thy troubled breath with that soul-energy, which wins all fights, unless it sink beneath its body's weight!'
>
> (Dante, *Inferno* XXIV)

28 December

Darling, I have now received the jumper and woollen socks you handmade for me. The jumper is so soft – I put it on immediately, with nothing else underneath so that I can feel the touch of your hands against my skin. The winter here is wet and windy, because of the sea storms, and we must put on layer upon layer to be able to get warm. I cannot thank you enough.

Today I finished the translation of the last songs. I have nothing to write on now. I don't have any paper left. I am keeping my fingers crossed that someone will bring some paper to me or to someone else here. I worked late last night. The little flame of the burning pine-stick flickered upon the wall frescos and made the apostles seem as if they were moving. It seemed everything was moving around me, my entire life, the angels' faces, people who once had lived here seeming to breathe around me, and then it felt like a silent dialogue was taking place between me and the apostles, or the once-believers who surround them. My friends are asleep. Xhako keeps complaining about his usual pain. Petro is barely alive. He is just breathing. Everything lies in an enormous bed of sadness; most of us are in an indescribable amount of pain.

A lonely bat circles around our beds as if performing a strange dance. Sotir raises his hand to seize it, but it escapes. Finally, over the silence, we hear Sotir cry out: 'Got it!' Everyone raised their sleepy heads. 'What did you catch?' asked Xhevo. 'A bat! Look at the little monster!' 'Give it a rest with those bats of yours, won't you?!', shouted Xhevo and went back to sleep muttering something. Sazan laughed. Sotir held the bat in his hand for a moment and then let it go: 'Go, fly away now … but careful not to wake Bulldog, or he'll kill you!' Silence reigned once more.

If you can, please send me some candles and some old notebooks. Ask Xhako's family or Petro's, Sotir's also. Perhaps someone has secured permission to visit and will soon be coming this way. Maybe someone has been provided with a permit and comes out to us.

Today I stood alone before the sea, looking at an empty, bland horizon. There were no ships, no small fishing boats either, no sea birds. In fact, the latter are rarely seen here because there is nothing for them to eat. I kept on gazing at the sea and thinking about all sorts of things …

I forgot to tell you that Kamberi has virtually lost his mind. Not long ago, his fiancée told him that their engagement was over and that she would live her life without him. She could not continue to pretend that she had a future with a convict. Poor Kamberi! Three days ago, he had some kind of seizure at the entrance of the monastery. He was in such a state, he could not believe what he had just learned. He loved her dearly. He let out a cry that wrenched our souls. There was foam coming out of his mouth. What a terrifying moment! He just didn't want to believe it. It really was like an epileptic fit. It was the first time I have seen a man with such an affliction. Later, Kamberi confirmed that he had suffered from epilepsy during his adolescence. The shock of the news had triggered a relapse after so many years, and he found himself on the floor.

His face went white and took on a corpse-like look. As he was falling to the ground, a tiny harmonica, which he kept always on him, fell out of his jacket pocket. He lay on that cold floor for about ten minutes and we did not know what to do. Skender had noticed the harmonica, and so he picked it up and started playing Kamberi's favourite tune. Surprisingly, as soon as the music filled the air, Kamberi moved and opened his eyes. He made a sign to Skender with his hand and Skender, pleased with this result, immediately handed him the instrument. Kamberi took it, got up and, staggering like a drunk, went towards the exit alone. We stood there saddened and in silence, thinking about what would happen next. Then all of a sudden, he started playing the harmonica and the beautiful sound reached every corner of the monastery.

What I told you just now happened the night before Christmas. Next day at lunchtime, we heard the bells ringing in the village. It must have been the call to Mass. The afternoon was cold and we stayed inside. We were all particularly sad. We could not help thinking of the world outside these walls on this joyous day, everyone gathered at home with their families. I thought of you, I thought of my mother who would not skip church even if she were sick.

How lonely and depressing to be so far away, totally isolated and confined to this island, not knowing one's destiny! As we were sitting there doing nothing, Sotir thought of improvising something to cheer us up. It was a little before sunset when he pulled out the Bible from underneath his pillow, threw a sheet over himself, and stood in front of one of the great frescos, just where the images of the apostles and saints were. Then, posing like a priest, taking on the importance of a man of the church, he turned to us and in a deep tremolo intoned: 'God said to Satan: "Did you notice my servant Job? For there is no one who is so honest and upright on earth, that he may fear God, and turn away from evil … behold, he is under thy dominion; but take not his life."'

As you know, Job from the Old Testament cursed the day of his birth because he wanted to put an end to the great punishments and ill-fortune that had struck him. Initially we laughed at his acting and his ridiculous costume, which consisted of a filthy sheet thrown over his body – an effort to make him look like a Roman or an ancient denizen of the Byzantine era. But soon enough, Job's story reminded us of our predicament: the misfortune, the unfair punishment and our doomed fate. Sotir, moving incessantly from left to right and back again along that apostolic frieze, continued:

> Why did I not die in the womb? … There the wicked cease to make trouble and there the weary find rest. The captives are completely at ease; they do not hear the voice of their oppressor. Why is light given to one burdened and life to those whose existence is bitter, who wait for death but it does not come? Why was I not hidden like a miscarried child? Like infants who never see daylight?*

His acting was passionately strange, until he came face-to-face with the image of John the Baptist holding his head. He suddenly paused. It was a spine-tingling scene. There was dead silence. We were watching first Sotir, then the faces of the apostles lit up by the candle flame … John the Baptist bearing his head and Sotir walking slowly, passing by each one of us with his extended hand, repeating: 'Now enjoy your forgetting of the persecutions that were inflicted! God extends his mercy to you! Even though you do not repent, the Lord understands the turbulence of your soul …' Then, when he was finished, he paused for a moment on his feet, without moving, confused, as if he had suddenly experienced enlightenment. Just like a statue, he stood silently there on the floor of the monastery. He almost passed over to infinity that night! As the moment ended, I imagined John the Baptist, along with his severed head, slowly retreating from that fresco.

Dearest Bruna, as I was translating Dante, line by line, I feel his prominence, why his craft is considered the greatest of them all, and then I say to myself: What a genius! I even sit close to Xhako and read the entire freshly translated paragraph to him, explaining everything about the part when Dante and Virgil wander in that big, dark cave. He has never heard of Dante and often asks me why I bother with him so much, but I tell him that Dante and we men are very much alike: we are the protagonists of his story, we are the mutilated lives that still flutter, trying to catch the light emanating from up there, the flickering light at the end of the tunnel.

So, naturally, I am reminded of the catacombs of Porto Palermo, of that citadel, in the galleries of which convicted elders, men, women and

---

* Part of Job's opening speech – Holman Christian Standard Bible.

children, about two hundred of us, were constantly watched over from above, from the tiny gaps between the stones where the light filtered through, feeling as if we were cavemen. It felt like the cave of Dionysius of Syracuse, the most terrible tyrant of all time, about whom Dante wrote in *Inferno* that he made violent men pay for their crimes by drowning them in boiling blood. I once told you about that cave that I saw in Syracuse, in the form of a giant ear, literally called 'the ear of Dionysius of Syracuse'.

Within that cave, the terrible tyrant of our time had imprisoned all who opposed him, his victims who were constantly being intercepted and overpowered for fear of revolt schemes that could overthrow and eventually kill him. In that cave, his guards recorded whatever sounded suspicious, heretical – feeding the paranoia that turned him into an animal, pouring his wrath on to us like a volcano. How is it possible, Bruna, that a human being can commit such crimes? Often, while I am translating, images of that cave resurface – a cave in which the beaten ones, the victims, carried the seeds of imminent revolt.

A week ago in the middle of the night, I was woken by lightning. Everyone else was still asleep. Light came flashing through the windows and fell on the fresco, illuminating the images of the saints. Astonishingly, in an instant under the lightning flashes, the saints seemed to come alive – they were no longer static there but appeared to be moving, their hands waving about, as if speaking in the language of the heavy rain. They seemed anxious, but why? Not because of us! And why were they crying out? Perhaps they were looking for their dearly departed monk ...

Two nights ago, I could not sleep. I got up and went out. There was a full moon, so bright that you could clearly see all the white and shadowed spots on its surface. What were they? I thought. Mountains, rivers? God knows. Is there life on the moon? A star-filled sky has always given me a sense of excitement; for a little while, looking at it, one forgets about all the suffering and mischief of this world. I felt like a true citizen of planet Earth as it should be, a planet without borders, void of political systems, a place where there is no war, no crime. There was dead silence, only the starry sky and me under that holy canopy, when suddenly I felt as if Giuseppina was singing the famous 'Ave Maria' of Schubert. It took me to another world; I forgot everything: it was you and me and no one else! I was with you! I find it slightly strange that my mind evoked exactly that piece, or is it perhaps that we know the singer? I put it down to the combined power of music and interpretation, something so extraordinary that allows us to escape reality for a few minutes and brings us together, to another land, where we do belong ...

There are many bats on this island. They hang upside down on tree branches in what seems to be their paradise. Some hang from the church beams or the beams of the monastery. Last night I watched them fly so close to me, in a dance-like motion, totally oblivious of my existence. Perhaps they are used now to peaceful people like us, the condemned, 'the greatest criminals of this world'. I could have caught them if I had stretched out my arm, if I wanted to, and let them go again ... but I didn't dream of disturbing their little ritual ...

Darling Bruna, a few days ago, another convict was transferred here. His name is Alexander; before the war he used to work as a journalist in Tirana. We must be of the same generation, but he looks like a seventy-year-old. They brought him here from another prison. Previously, he had been part of Maliq's forced labour camp in charge of drying up the infamous bog. He could barely stand up; on top of his obvious frailty, he is a diabetic. He looked like a walking corpse.

We immediately took care of him. He seemed to be very surprised that they had brought him to this particular island. The second night, we gathered around him and he told us why he had been convicted. He had been working for more than a year like an animal, in Maliq. He told us that there were hundreds of convicts digging this long canal daily, from dawn to dusk. He even told us the story of one man whom the supervising soldiers had tried to bury alive right there, in front of other prisoners. It sounded unreal, but he swore to us that it was true and that he had seen it with his own eyes. Luckily, someone had notified the lieutenant, who came running and spoke fiercely to the two soldiers who had almost buried the poor man up to his throat. He was gasping for air. He was then pulled out of there, escaping his imminent death. I again thought of Dostoyevsky's *The House of the Dead*. The master was also convicted for his political views and worked for four years in the Siberian labour camps, an experience about which he would later testify. Oh sweetie, I do not want to sadden you with these stories, but I tell you everything because I just can't keep it all to myself.

Additionally, during the fascist era, Alexander had been exiled to the island of Ventotene, where he had met many Italian revolutionaries as well as a group of Albanians who had participated in the Spanish Civil War. It is striking that after having endured most of his sentence on one island, he is sent to another island, suffering the same punishment; reduced to skin and bone and seriously ill. I wonder why they do that. I'm afraid he will not live much longer … One day, with that hoarse voice of his, he sang one of the Ventotene camp songs called 'O bella, ciao' … I had not heard that song before. How beautiful? It penetrated my soul! He sang and when it was over, he wept.

> One morning I woke up / and I found the invaders /
> O partisan, take me away / because I feel I shall die!

My dear, my shoulder still hurts, especially when it rains. It wakes me up in the middle of the night at times and I need to be sure not to rest on it, otherwise the pain is greater. To forget about the pain, I think about you. I start to count the hours, days, months, years of isolation that remain until, one day, the door will open, and I will run to you. Sometimes, while sleeping, when I turn on the other side, the pain is so great that I suddenly wake up breathless. However, I hope that the fracture is slowly healing, and it will gradually regain normal function.

As I started translating the last song, song thirty-four, I was very impressed by a fragment where Dante wrote: 'I did not die, nor yet remained alive; think for thyself now, hast thou any wit, what I became, of both of these deprived'.

Ah, what a verse! The dehumanization – so profound that people feel as if they are alive and dead at the same time, or dead-alive. It seems paradoxical, but many locked up in terrible prisons are dead-alive, and few are those who manage to escape this death that haunts them like a second shadow and eventually pins them down until there is nothing but silence. Yet some manage to overcome fear, pain, physical suffering and constant violence, pulled up by a force that suddenly emerges from within, their soul, and their thoughts. Without this force, we would all be 'the living dead'.

One evening, it was raining heavily. Sefer was very sad because his wife's request to visit him had been rejected again. He was angry and kept wandering around the monastery hall, like a wounded bull. He walked up and down, shouting abuse and screaming, and suddenly pushed open the heavy door and went out into the pouring rain. He pulled off his jumper, then his shoes, his pants, and then everything, and naked as he was, began to yell at Bulldog, who was watching him from a distance, his automatic rifle in his hands: 'Tell me, what have I done to you? Why don't you let my wife visit me? Why am I even here? Because I fought so hard? Aren't my wounds and my brother's life enough?' Protected, wearing his dark raincoat, Bulldog only laughed at his nakedness and mocked him: 'Be careful not to get your butt wet!'

Suddenly, he slammed back the rod of the automatic, maybe to intimidate him, and Sotir and I rushed to take Sefer inside. We dragged him back naked, collecting up his clothes and muddy shoes, but he continued to yell at Bulldog: 'Look, look at this wound so it burns into your memory! This was my fight, not yours!' In the distance, Bulldog laughed constantly. It was a painful, unforgettable scene. Finally, we got inside. My dearest, ours is another life. Whatever we do, however loud our voices, who will hear us here? Yet we will survive!

At midnight when the rain stopped, the bats, scared and tossed about by the great wind, came around beating their wings and crying in despair. Two of them collided with the window, their force breaking the glass into the smallest pieces.

Last night I had a strange dream, darling. I was sleeping when a voice whispered to me. I opened my eyes and under the moonlight, entering the monastery, I saw a shadow approaching and leaning over me. 'Who are you?', I asked. 'I'm Beso, Professor', he replied. 'What are you doing here?' 'Get up', he said, 'I have come to get you!' 'To go where?' 'Home! Follow me … don't make any noise.' I got up. The others were sleeping. It was such a chilly night. I got out and followed him to the shore, where he motioned me to board the boat behind him. And I jumped into it. He paddled away quickly, the oars churning, and we were halfway to the other shore when, unexpectedly, a floodlight from the island hit us. It was like a Cyclops eye. Beso paddled as hard as he could, to try and get out of the light, but it still found us. At the same time, someone opened fire. Bullets were whistling around the boat. Beso got wounded. We were near the shore when Beso groaned, grabbed his throat to stop the massive bleeding and then collapsed to the ground. 'I can't believe it!', I cried. And then I woke up … Ah, dear, I am now scared for his life. You never know what might have happened to him!

One more thing, sweetheart: in your last letter you wrote that you went past the high school and met my good friend Pashk; that you saw my students, the young ones, in groups and talking quietly. You say that they seemed a bit frightened? Maybe. I'm convinced they must have learned what really happened to me. I remember the first year of school opening after the war, when I was constantly surrounded by those young inquisitive minds, my students asking dozens of questions. I was looking on an entirely new world. They had dreamy eyes and were always smiling, delighted with the new life of freedom arising right in front of them. I always think of them while translating Dante. I follow Dante's path when he is with Virgil – they finally find that stairway to climb up from the dark cavern to life and light, up there, where they will see the stars, on the other side of the Earth. At the triumphant finish, for whatever reason, I see the students' faces, Ludovik's eyes, this energetic young man, as stubborn as he was wise, always looking further ahead. I remember once, during one of my lectures about the Roman Emperors in class, I explained how Caligula declared his horse as a senator. His knowledge and argument about the paralyzing effect of tyranny on the progress of any human society, and the vital need for freedom so society can move toward civilization, was impressive.

I wonder, Bruna, whether I will ever get back to them. Whether I will ever be able to speak to my students again. I am convinced that none of them thinks I deserve this punishment. Yet, I wish and hope that, out of all that is happening to me, they will learn something. I would like it if they read and learned something from the *Inferno* that I am translating, because *Inferno* has taught great lessons to the entire world, and Dante is one of the greatest humanists who ever lived.

I will end this long letter to you here, my dearest, by citing what Victor Hugo once said about Dante. I was in Turin when I first read this passage where Hugo mentions two of the greatest giants of literature, Dante and Shakespeare: he said that in Shakespeare, we see real people; in Dante, a spectral version of them. Of Dante, he wrote something like this:

> Dante has mentally conceived the abyss. He has made the epic poem of spectres. He rends the earth; in the terrible hole he has made, he puts Satan. Then he pushes through Purgatory up to Heaven. Where all end, Dante begins. Dante is beyond man; beyond, not without – a singular proposition which, however, has nothing contradictory in it, the soul being a prolongation of man into the indefinite. Dante twists all light and shade into a terrifying spiral; it descends, then it ascends. Wonderful architecture, never previously conceived of! At the threshold is the sacred mist; across the entrance is stretched the corpse of Hope; all that you perceive beyond is night. The infinite anguish is sobbing somewhere in the invisible darkness. You lean over this gulf-poem. Is it a crater?

Yes, my love, a crater, a giant crater … The abyss that Dante created into which, unaware, we have fallen. Can we get out of it? Hugo talks about the corpse of Hope, but I believe the opposite. I believe that hope survives. I believe that, in the name of love, we will overcome the circles of hell on earth …

I pour all my longing for you into a big kiss and send it away with this letter. Give my mother a big hug from me, Bruna.

Fred

'*Morituri te salutant*' … 'Those who go to die, greet you'

* * *

The old stove of the monastery burns the last pieces of wood. It is freezing. Evening has fallen on the island. Suddenly a great howling wind hits the monastery's walls, its door and and window. It's the end of the year. Lying down, the convicts try to catch some sleep. One of them moans under an old lantern. The rest look at each other, wishing for a better year: one that enters on the right foot, that brings something good and new, even though hope has almost died.

'There is nothing left, but to dream!', says Sotir looking at Kamberi before closing his eyes.

Then dead silence, just the echo of the wind. No one dares to close their eyes. No one dares to dream. What dream? Dreams have faded away. Absurd to dream in here. All they are left with is to look their doomed fate in the eye …

The morning comes with the deafening noise of firing arms. One shot and then another.

'What's going on?', Sazan asks.

Everyone jumps from their beds, while Sotir approaches the window and, suddenly, lets out a child-like cry of delight: 'It's snowing!'

Yet another shot pierces the sky. The convicts run to the door, while Bulldog, laughing and yelling, goes: 'I killed him! I killed the bastard!'

The guards have been shooting wild rabbits that had come out of the bushes and jumped over the snow, scared by the noise. The snow has covered everything.

A miracle of nature and, here and there, stains of fresh blood.

Triumphant, Bulldog, holding up three rabbits, shows off to the convicts.

1 January. A new year has already entered with a bloody snow …

* * *

# THE TWELFTH LETTER

> I really saw, and still I seem to see it, a trunk without a head, which moved along, as moved the others of the mournful herd; and by the hair it held the severed head, which, hanging like a lantern from its hand, was saying as it gazed at us: 'O me!'
>
> (Dante, *Inferno* XXVIII)

12 February 1958

My dearest Bruna: finally, I finished translating *Inferno*. The last line of the entire piece goes like this: '*E quindi uschimmo a veder le stelle*' … 'Hence we came out, and saw again the stars'.

It was an immense pleasure and a torture at the same time, all these months, this long year living in here. I wanted to tell you that while working on it, in the twenty-second song, I came across two lines which I will always remember: 'With the ten demons we were going on; ah, the fierce company!'

It is hard not to make the analogy with the demons that keep us confined here. Of course, not all of them are demons, but it suffices that those on top be demons for life to become a nightmare. In fact, I even dreamed about a similar thing happening and I got so scared, I asked myself: How long will the power of these demons last?! Ah Bruna, I'm going to write now about something I've hesitated to mention before, but

I really need to tell you, because you are the only soul I can tell about all the things that hurt me in this life as well as all those that make me happy. While being interrogated, as they torture you no end, you think that at some point they will kill you; you are nothing but a number to them. So, I once asked myself: Why not give in, since Bruna is waiting for me. Tell them what they want to hear and get out of this dark hole. But then I thought: What will Bruna think of me? Will I ever be able to look her in the eye? Will I have the courage to tell her the truth? Then my mother's face appeared. I was stepping from all that darkness into the light and, for a moment, it felt like the sunlight blinded me, but soon my mother's figure appeared in front of me and I stopped right in front of her. She seemed frozen as she said, 'You too, son? How did that happen?' I looked down for a moment and when I looked up again she had vanished, as if by a holy spirit or magic, leaving me all alone, abandoned, in the middle of that wide road. I then turned around and said to myself: Go back into the darkness; go back to hell.

Dear Bruna, when I finished translating the last song, instead of cheering, I felt really sad. That is because Dante's words had become necessary to me, as they resembled a path towards the light. This song is the most powerful of the entire *Divine Comedy*. The man finds himself in it, his life, the history in general, finds the great evil, the one that kills the soul and then the body. This evil that puts down the weak and makes him his slave, his captive. Dante's *Inferno* is over, my dear, but hell here goes on. I will send the final song to you with Xhako's wife, who will be visiting at the end of this month. Do you know what Dante's last words are? Read it, darling, as there is nothing more beautiful and dramatic:

> My Leader then, and I, in order to regain the world of light, entered upon that dark and hidden path; and, without caring for repose, went up, he going on ahead, and I behind, till through a rounded opening I beheld some of the lovely things the sky contains; thence we came out, and saw again the stars.

How lovely to walk out into the light – something I always dream of in this eternal darkness that surrounds us, not knowing if this terrible journey will ever come to an end! One reads Dante and automatically thinks of what it means to be covered by that white light of life. Will I live to see the day when I walk out of this dark tunnel and step into that light? Sefer always gives me courage, whereas Xhako always repeats that life is simply a game and that we should not be feeling sorrow but rather be happy every moment we are alive, even in hell, because what matters is not isolation, lack of basic freedom, but to feel free within yourself, to feel free even when locked up, even when they forbid you to speak. To think freely even when you are not physically free, because no one can handcuff the kind of freedom that you house within. Am I free though, if I cannot be with you? I do not believe so. For you are my freedom! …

Bruna, I always wonder how Dante managed to live in exile for so long until his death in Ravenna on that September day of 1321. I try to imagine his death, tired of that infinite wandering, always fleeing, feeling persecuted and lonely. I went to Ravenna only once. I remember we stayed in the city square. It was raining. My Italian friend asked me whether I could see the old house further down the road and told me that it was thought that Dante had died there. I looked at the closed windows and imagined the last time Dante saw the light of day coming through. What a great burden to die away from your home country, far from the yard where you have spent your childhood and your youth, where everyone you have ever loved lives! Nevertheless, Dante believed in paradise. Is paradise possible for man? Hard to say! What's truly remarkable is that he had imagined hell on earth. The hell of yesterday and the one that was yet to come … Have we not lived through hell also – a twentieth-century hell that has seen millions and millions of dead, wounded and mutilated? Two big wars did not suffice for this world to understand the meaning of true hell, and now, a new war is on the horizon.

Remember Stefan, the one who managed to return alive from Mauthauzen? The fellow we met one day at Shehnaz who told us all his Calvary: the life in the Nazi camp and his survival calendar, the extermination kilns and the black smoke rising up as if it were a sign of the whole world's funeral? He was one of the few remaining alive from that greatest of human massacres; the hell created by men to kill men! Through *Inferno*, Dante will always be reminding us of what we are capable …

Enough of this dark talk, Bruna; I want to tell you about something joyous! Three days ago, two beautiful, white pelicans landed on the island. We followed them around the island as they were flying low until they stopped near the church belfry. We thought that they would perhaps stay. They would be such good company! For the rest of the day and the next few days, they flew around, checked out the woods nearby, and returned with branches in their beaks as if they were trying to set up nest. It was enough to make us forget that we were in gaol for a moment. They made many trips, beating their big wings and reminding us of the meaning of genesis, birth, where we all come from. A nest was rising. And that's all it takes to make us happy here.

I dreamed of you the other night, Bruna. It was early afternoon when I saw you rushing towards me, happy, through the main door. You hugged me tight and I asked you what had happened. 'I am pregnant!', you said, pressing the side of your head against my chest. I couldn't breathe for a second. It was the best news I had ever heard. And then you took my hand and placed it on the bottom of your belly, pressed it against your warm body and whispered: 'I felt it today, I heard it … the baby is moving! Can you feel it?' I went down on my knees and put my ear right next to where you were pointing. I wanted to hear that magic, wondrous heartbeat. I cannot describe how happy I felt! … But then, there was lightning on the island and I woke up …

'*Pax in terra hominibus bonae voluntatis*' … 'Peace on earth to men of good will!'

# EPILOGUE

> 'So may your memory never fly away from human minds in that first world of ours, but rather under many suns survive …'
>
> (Dante, *Inferno* XXIX)

Far away, at the shore, appeared a woman's silhouette, barely holding up because of the strong winds on that cold winter's day. Through the heavy wooden door of the monastery, at first emerged Xhako then Sefer and then all the convicts, one by one. They watched Rrapush who helped the woman board the boat and beat his paddles as fast as he could. Who was this woman? The silence was deafening. Her silhouette was fast approaching. Nobody knew her, nobody had seen her before.

'Who is she?' They looked at each other as if someone would have the answer. 'Sotir's sister!', whispered Sefer. 'No, it isn't Sotir's sister.' 'Who is she, then?' They looked at each other, lifting their shoulders. 'Might it be Bruna?' 'How could it be Bruna? Haven't they told her?'

The little boat was fast approaching. Her eyes were searching for her husband. She looked confused and surprised not to have distinguished her husband among these sad and silent creatures. Rrapush let go of her arm and, while walking away, murmured: 'Lady, I will be back to fetch you in two hours!' He made a sign to the soldier with whom they came to the monastery. Another soldier got closer to the woman.

'Rrapush, wait!', she yelled, afraid of what she could hear. Where was her loved one, where?

'Where is my husband?', she asked the soldier, who was carefully reading her permission to visit. He finished reading it, folded the permit slowly and gave her a dirty and angry look. 'Tell me, what happened to him!' Sefer got a step closer to her. 'Bruna?' 'Yes!', she said with a faint voice. Sefer embraced her gently.

'Bruna, yesterday they came and took him away for some kind of trial in Tirana.' 'Took him out of here again?' 'Yes, Bruna … you know, when you are in gaol, trouble never finishes!' Bruna stood a frozen moment and felt his heart breaking while giving her the news. A tear slipped away, but she wiped it off immediately. 'You need to leave now!', the lieutenant mumbled. Shocked as she was, she gave him a dirty look, while Sefer pushed her away. 'His clothes are here … we hope he will return but can never be sure.'

Bruna lowered the sack she was holding and offered it to Xhako. 'You can keep it … there is some food inside.' Then, casting a long, silent look over the monastery, the church, the tall pines, and the stumpy bushes, she turned her head in the direction of the approaching soldier, as if to say goodbye, even though he was looking at her with contempt. Sefer followed her to the boat and, before she boarded, he secretly handed Bruna a letter which she quickly hid away before anyone noticed. 'He gave it to me for you, before he left …' She smiled painfully and boarded the boat. The sky thundered. It seemed that it was going to rain. The prisoners, gathered together, followed the disappearing silhouette of the young woman who did not meet her beloved husband one last time.

Riding on the back of a truck, hardly able to keep her balance because of the fierce winds, Bruna opened the letter with her trembling hands and began to read, with her vision clouded by tears:

> 21 March
>
> Dearest Bruna, now that I've finished *Inferno*, I see life differently. I have become someone else, a man who is thankful to God for having met Dante again, here, on this forgotten island. Who would have thought that one day I would be here translating this work? That I would live every day of my life in the company of this masterpiece? Tell me! Dante taught me how to understand this ephemeral life.

It sounds perhaps strange, but Dante kept me on my feet, kept me alive, breathing. Night after night, awake and in my sleep, in my dreams and nightmares. Unlike my friends here, I found something to cling into, I found a certain kind of courage within those pages, in what Dante wrote, the unfortunate poet who, in return, by coming to me, to us, survived death, in this camp where freedom is constantly handcuffed. Dante removed the shackles of my feet as he made me realize that there are bigger tragedies in the life of a man and that of a nation, and that once you overcome this tragedy, life begins once again, stronger, more beautiful …

I know, my love, that you suffer more than me, though with my mind, I have walked through all circles of Hell, finally understanding what a man is, a human being, understanding humanity, lack of freedom and the real value of human love. I often wondered: Has human nature been the same since the dawn of time? Has man been created to destroy? To ruin cities, civilizations, all the good ever created by others before him? To foster a society where the son kills his father, neighbours kill each other, a society which rejoices over crime? It begs the questions: Where did Nero come from, where did Dionysius of Syracuse of Sicily and others – criminals, dictators, the greatest violators of freedom – come from? And yet, I want to believe that all men are not evil. Dante, too, despite it all, trusted in man and in love. I have faith in both. Men can be brought up differently, built differently through culture, poetry, music and art. Among other things, in the last song, Dante wrote: '"Hold on tight", my Master said, breathing like a man that is being chased. "Up the stairs like this we will climb to leave behind a place of so much evil." Then, through an opening in the rock he issued, and, after seating me upon its edge, over toward me advanced his cautious step.'

Bruna dearest, the day I leave this island and return to you, the day I truly return from hell and fall into the arms of your love, a love beyond paradise, our world will be entirely different. We will know full well how to build our lives, enjoy our children and have a different future. The winter we are living through is a severe one, full of lightning bolts that destroy people's lives, and yet, I have faith. Dante had faith in the future. I am confident that spring will come, and we will be able to enjoy our lives at last. This madness will pass. Take a look at the verses I wrote last night in the dim light of the burning pine, which I titled 'Midnight at the End of March'. Here's what I wrote:

> It was midnight when someone knocked:
> 'Hurry up! I am Death, I've come to pick you up!'
> Breathless I asked:
> 'Right now? … Oh, no!'
> And the door on its face I shut.
> A sound like half of the world collapsed.
> 'What was it?', half-asleep you asked
> when to bed I returned.
> 'The wind, just the wind', I whispered,
> and fell asleep in your arms as if for the last time,
> while you whispered in your dreams,
> I am sure, something about love:
> as if we soaked in the morning sun
> I had marvelled over you until dawn,
> careful not to wake you up,
> holding you on the tip of my burning lips
> and kissed you a thousand times
> inside my chest, a thousand butterflies.
> I felt the streams of blood flowing,
> and an oracle's voice calling me.

Then, in the morning to you I said:
'Wake up, my love, plum trees have blossomed
like the flowers on your wedding dress,
wake up to lengthen the day
and to make shorter the night,
wake up so we embrace again our friends,
and those who have made us suffer to the end,
hate in this world of darkness holds no place,
so come, I want to hold you in my arms,
so that together we can walk to the other end of
the world,
where there are no more horizons,
with a rose upon my chest,
'till my very last day, 'till the very end …'

My darling, I hold you very tightly and kiss you.
'*Lux in tenebris*' … 'Light in the depth of the darkness'

* * *

And this letter marks the end of the correspondence of the political prisoner, Fred Çoba. He did not return to the island of Zaratha, and his wife's letters, which seem to have been hidden in the monastery, were not found. The famous epistle kept hidden and safe by his wife was published forty years later, when the dictatorship of Enver Hoxha was overthrown. Former prisoners of that camp still remember the professor of literature who sang 'O bella, ciao' so beautifully. Alexander died a month after his release. Two years later, Sefer was released and invited to join the army but he refused and went to work at a brick factory. A new contingent of sickly prisoners arrived on the island at the end of spring and the island was populated again. The poet continued to write his poems and often got lost in the forest of Zaratha where he lay convulsing, with no one nearby to help, while Sotir continued to recite Pirandello's verses as if he were giving his graduation performance in Rome. He was later transferred to a psychiatric ward, where he continued to declare that Alexander Moisi was his prophet.

Xhevo was released after ten years of imprisonment and immediately sent to exile. Sazan did not enjoy life in freedom. One year after his release, he died of tuberculosis at a small village in Myzeqe. The Dante Alighieri Association reopened in Tirana in the last years of the twentieth century. A few years later, all of the characters of the Zaratha camp had died – former convicts and inquisitors. Dante and his masterpiece outlived everyone, continuing his journey towards enlightenment, through the inevitable walk from darkness to human light.

# AFTERWORD

## *ZARATHA'S EPISTOLARY*: ITS MAKING AND HISTORICAL TRUTH

I was first introduced to Dante's *Divine Comedy* during my university years. We had to read this famous work as part of our coursework. My professor of early medieval and medieval literature, Myzafer Xhaxhiu, spoke often and with an extraordinary passion about Dante and Beatrice. So much so, he looked pathetic and we, in fact, thought that he was a prisoner of their world, which made him look different from the others. He tried in vain to make us read Dante: his *Inferno*, his *Purgatory* and his *Paradise*. At the time, all we could think of was foreign music: the Beatles, Celentano, Battisti, and other European bands and singers of the 1960s. Dante was hard to understand and so we almost ignored it and forgot all about it later. Years would go by and, in my travels, I would visit Florence. A friend of mine, an Albanian painter, suggested that we visit Dante's house. As we were getting through the door, he pointed to another building, almost fifty metres away from Dante's house, telling me that there once stood the house of Dante's great love, Beatrice. Later, while writing an article about Botticelli, I would come across numerous wonderful illustrations of the *Divine Comedy*, most of which in black and white. Another world appeared in front of my eyes: human bodies falling from above or floating in the circles of Hell, for Hell constitutes undoubtedly the most thought-provoking and disturbing sequence of those drawings. We have, of course, surely seen the face of indescribable torture, arbitrary imprisonment and lynching of human beings on this side of the world, followed by the political changes in Albania with the falling of the totalitarian regime in the 1990s; as in all other Eastern European countries, the dictatorship era came to an end. It was then that we started to grasp our shocking reality, the severity of crime, of violence and the magnitude of violation of free speech and freedom in general. Yet, it was not until reading an article in one of the Albanian newspapers about the well-known Latin language expert, Pashko Gjeçi, and then the story of Mark Ndoja, that I learned about the existence of a small island near Vlora Bay, called Zvërnec, somewhat hidden from the world, where some of the most despicable crimes had been committed. Unlike Pashko Gjeci who translated *Inferno* after his release from prison, when he began teaching Italian Renaissance literature at the university, Mark Ndoja had begun to translate it while in prison. In that script, I read a few passages from a letter that he had sent to his wife, talking about the difficulties related to translating Dante, which prompted me to write this book in an epistolary form because of this unique fact: a man going through hell while translating Dante's *Inferno*! What an extraordinary circumstance! And then I began to really read Dante, especially *Inferno* – to imagine Hell's circles, his journey, the connection with the great poet Virgil, as well as the various art history figures whom they encounter during that long and fearsome journey. Dante imagined Hell in the form of a funnel that descended deep into the earth; the more you descend, the narrower the path. There, together with his companion, somewhere in a hollow part, they find a set of subordinate stairs to finally climb to the light, to see the glorious sky and to ascend to Purgatory and then to Paradise where he will meet with his Beatrice.

As I was writing this epistolary, many different images played in my mind. First, the images of an early trip to Zvërnec when I was a filmmaker: on that idyllic island, in that 'natural paradise', I saw the empty church and the silent monastery where no traces of former political prisoners could be found. Kasem Trebeshina, Tuk Jakova, Mark Ndoja, Spiro Gjoka and many other Albanian intellectuals had spent a considerable time in this terrible prison. It was also while I was visiting that I recalled the stories told by my good friend, Henrik Gjoka, about a time when he and his grandmother walked along the seaside all the way from Vlora to the lagoon of Zvërnec, just so that they could spend one or two days among the prisoners, with their loved ones.

Here we are: the landscape, the historical characters, their dramas, which blended in my mind with the images that I had seen in the citadel of Ali Pasha at Tepelena along the Ionian coast, in that Venetian fortress, in the cells of which were once held some two hundred prisoners and convicts – men, women, children. A hell, similar to Dante's *Inferno.* Those men, though surrounded by the sea, locked in the dark, were not allowed to see the sea. Rather, they could hear the waves and the screaming of the sea birds roaming the sky that remained unseen to them. Some of those who had been in Zvërnec had previously been held in other camps, such as Porto Palermo, Tepelena and elsewhere.

By chance, during my high school years, I knew the daughter of Mark Ndoja, Marinta. We lived in the same neighbourhood, but I did not know then that she was the daughter of the secretary of the League of Writers Academy, who had been condemned and sent to Zvërnec. After the first publication of this book, I had the opportunity to learn more of her story. Marinta had gone through the same Calvary as my friend Henrik Gjoka; she too, along with her mother and brother, had followed the route through the coastal marshland to get to Zvërnec to see her father. She told me that once, straggling some way behind her mother and brother, she was almost sucked under by the mud. I imagine the moment when an adolescent girl, despairing that her life was coming to an untimely end, was saved only by an almighty force: her love for her father. This girl who was ordered to strip naked before the guards at the entry point, to prove that she was hiding no weapons … And she remembered the apples that she had quickly bundled up for her father on the day he was arrested, when he was taken to be imprisoned. Before having received her testimony, I had already written in this epistolary about apples for the prisoners.

After the first publication of this book, another friend of mine, Tuk Jakova's daughter, gave me a book comprising letters that her father had sent to his wife Mita. I read them on the plane on my way back to Paris, details which gave me goose bumps passing through skies blurred from my tears. Without a doubt, they were disturbing and inspiring letters at the same time. Upon reading them, I realized that my encounter was almost a carbon copy of that painful reality, which became part of Dante's imaginary world – a man who closed his eyes far away from his own land, condemned to exile until his death in 1321. No doubt, great works are born from great pain …

www.ingramcontent.com/pod-product-compliance
Ingram Content Group UK Ltd.
Pitfield, Milton Keynes, MK11 3LW, UK
UKHW040243300726
14061UKWH00002BD/139

9 781925 801743